Maurice Richard
RELUCTANT HERO

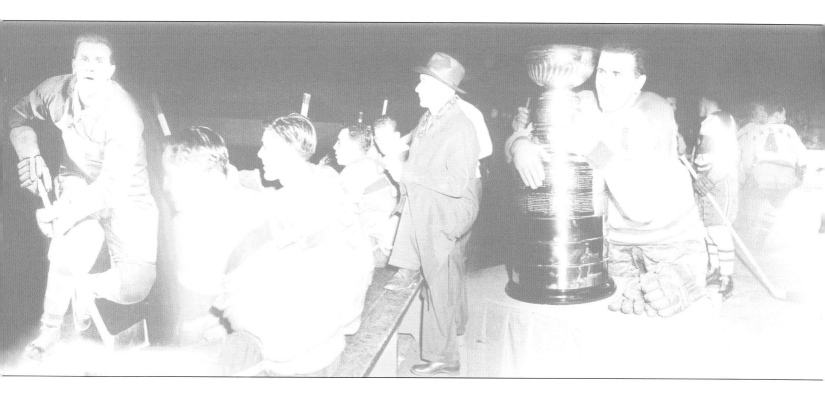

MAURICE RICHARD

R E L U C T A N T   H E R O

Chrys Goyens | Frank Orr
with Jean-Luc Duguay

TPP / TEAM POWER
PUBLISHING INC.
toronto montréal

Published By Team Power Publishing Inc., a division of Team Power Enterprises Inc.

Publisher Allan Turowetz

Editor in Chief Chrys Goyens

Creative Director Julie Desilets

Co-ordinator | Researcher Geneviève Desrosiers

Graphic Designers Julie Desilets, Nathalie Michaud

Computer Graphics Patrick Dupuis

Colour Separation | Films | Printing Quebecor World Graphique-Couleur

Binding Reliure Montréal

Canadian Cataloguing In Publication Data

Goyens, Chrys, 1949-
Maurice Richard: Reluctant Hero
Issued also in French under title: Maurice Richard : héros malgré lui
Includes bibliographical references.

ISBN 0-9686220-4-6

1. Richard, Maurice, 1921- 2000 2. Hockey players – Quebec (Province).
– Biography I. Orr, Frank, 1936- II. Title.

GV848.5.R5G69 2000   796.962'092   C00-901451-9

Legal deposit, fourth quarter, 2000
National Library of Canada
Bibliothèque nationale du Québec

C O N T E N T S

As a young boy growing up in Montreal, I shared a hero with hundreds of thousands of Quebeckers and Canadians. He was the best French-Canadian hockey player who had ever lived, and his exploits were legion.

He was also my brother.

Maurice was almost 15 years my senior, which meant that we could not enjoy a conventional relationship between brothers; he married the year I began elementary school. As I got older, and my own hockey talents surfaced, however, big brother took a long distance interest in me.

And then, one day, we were teammates. Like a select group of young Quebeckers who grew up listening on radio to the fantastic deeds Maurice fashioned at the Forum and other National Hockey League arenas, I suddenly found myself in the same dressing room.

Nothing changed, he was still my hero and much larger than life. Jean Béliveau, Bernard Geoffrion, Jean-Guy Talbot, Claude Provost, Dickie Moore, Phil Goyette; we all shared the experience of becoming teammates with the *Idole d'un peuple*.

And, while we were "equals" in the sense of teammates and, eventually, stars in our own right and Hall of Famers much later, Maurice was in a place none of us could reach.

Only he has ever stood on that very special pedestal. Only he ever will.

He was the Rocket, and this book gives this generation an idea of what he meant to all of us.

Henri Richard

Dear Maurice

You, whose name became a shining light
   and whose exploits were legendary;
You, who were the passion and intensity of hockey
   incarnate for so many years;
You, whose values and actions
   inspired many generations;
You, who wore No. 9, the red-white-and-blue, and the "C",
   with authenticity and an unshakeable team spirit;
You, whose sublimation of self
   and the desire to win were the only law;
You, who shared a special bond with your fans
   and were so giving of yourself;
You, who gave true meaning to the word "Canadiens"
   and who blazed the path of a team's destiny;
You, who were a humble man,
   a doting father and a magical player;
Your history must be written and read,
   for it is the wellspring of our commitment.

Thank you, Rocket.

Pierre Boivin
President, Club de hockey Canadien

Les Canadiens

L'HISTOIRE SE JOUE CHAQUE FOIS

HISTORY WITH EVERY STRIDE

Maurice *Rocket* Richard had just passed away on that last Saturday afternoon in May and the rest of the weekend had many Quebec television stations, especially those in the French language, turn to All-Richard, All-the-Time programming.

Talking heads with sports, cultural and socio-political backgrounds scrambled like fighter pilots as special broadcasts were cobbled together and brought to air. Channel surfing resulted in the same career highlights segments appearing all across the spectrum, with the same old scratchy kinescopes showing the Rocket whip a twenty-foot wrister past Don Simmons (Boston goalie, left-handed, a rarity in those days), deke Chuck Rayner of the Rangers on a back-hand (a signature Josef Stalin back-combed pompadour), circle the net in Toronto (in colour, yet) and score the last goal of his career (Game Three of the 1960 final, Maple Leaf Gardens, Johnny Bower).

The obligatory Richard Riot footage aired, the same posters (in French) declaring to posterity that *Campbell is a pig* waved by crowds of young French-Canadians – they would become francophones and *Québécois* later – taunting (the then) majority English police force.

Those images would blur in the background as sports experts two generations removed from Maurice Richard's National Hockey League tried to make sense of the profound loss felt by Quebeckers and, as witnessed by the outpouring of emotion from the other nine provinces (Don Cherry: *"The Rocket was our hero, too"*), and Canadians from coast-to-coast.

The word icon was used a lot.

In the midst of this, the Réseau des Sports, TSN's French-language sister network, was conducting its umpteenth special when the show's *host du jour* turned to his "sports expert", a well-known, intelligent and experienced hockey coach in his early thirties.

"You know," the expert said, echoing the mood of the weekend, *"I was too young. I never saw the Rocket play."*

An astounding revelation to a hockey nation built on television coverage of our favourite sport; but one which went a long way toward beginning to establish the context for the *Search for Rocket's popularity.*

Maurice *Rocket* Richard retired on September 15, 1960, two hockey generations ago. He was thirty-nine years old then, and would live another thirty-nine years in retirement, a period usually conducive to collective amnesia.

While Richard enjoyed his post-hockey life, Wayne Gretzky (*né 1961*) and Mario Lemieux (*né 1965*) would take their first teetering steps on skates, grow up and play their entire careers on television in front of millions of adoring fans, *and then retire themselves.* Bobby Orr and Guy Lafleur's careers would come and go, as would the Soviet-Canada Summit Series of 1972, Canada Cups in the 1970s, '80s and '90s, and the first Olympic Games experiment in Japan with NHL players, all watershed events in the development of the sport as we now know it.

Who was this man whom *nobody* saw play, and who earned ovations everywhere he went for four decades after his career ended?

Who was this icon?

What did he mean to the game?

This book will reacquaint you with the phenomenon that was No. 9, *as seen by* the hockey executives, opponents, teammates, referees and media observers who were there when he lit up National Hockey League rinks in hockey's Golden Age.

Frank Selke and Conn Smythe in the executive suite, players on both sides of the puck, referees like Red Storey, Bill Chadwick and Frank Udvari, all had opinions on the Richard phenomenon.

And it is fitting that we turn to the journalists, in their own voices as they spoke or wrote then, as the framework for this book: Scott Young, Milt Dunnell, George Dulmage and Jim Coleman in Toronto, or the Montreal contingent of Charles Mayer, Paul Parizeau, Louis Chantigny, Marcel Desjardins, Marc Thibeault, Rocky Brisebois, Zotique Lespérance and Jacques Beauchamp on the French side, as well as the English press corps of Baz O'Meara, Elmer Ferguson, Dink Carroll, Vern DeGeer, Andy O'Brien and Red Fisher.

They saw the Rocket play, and reported on his career every day.

BEGINNINGS

*H*e came from nowhere. Maurice Richard,

the greatest of the Lions in Winter, arrived

on the scene in the fall of 1942 with little

fanfare and fewer expectations, partially because

Montreal Canadiens fans had learned to aim low

after more than a decade of futility. The team had

not won a Stanley Cup since the halcyon days of

Howie Morenz, Aurel Joliat and George Hainsworth in

1930-31. Later on in team history, Jean Béliveau's ascen-

sion to the scene would become a three-year-long soap opera,

and Guy Lafleur's arrival the culmination of a series of astute

management moves by Sam Pollock. 9

But, when Joseph Henri Maurice Richard joined the National Hockey League Montreal Canadiens for training camp in 1942, he was just another winger trying to win a spot on a mediocre team. At that, he bore the tag of "fragile" player, who had endured an average season with the junior Verdun Maple Leafs in 1939-40, and then missed most of the ensuing two campaigns with the Canadiens of the Quebec Senior League because of injuries.

Years later, Richard confided to veteran sportswriter, Andy O'Brien: *"I still can't figure what Canadiens saw in me to offer me that first pro contract. I was hopelessly awkward and fragile. It seemed I was always on my ass or in the hospital."*

Toe Blake, who would become his linemate on the Punch Line, and then his coach, concurred at the time. *"I don't think Maurice Richard is going to make it; this league is just too tough on him,"* Blake said.

Frank Selke would be Maurice Richard's boss for most of his NHL career. For the first five years of Richard's sojourn in the top pro league, however, he was a respectful opponent as the number two hockey man in Toronto.

"He was playing in junior A hockey with the Verdun Maple Leafs, when I was acting manager of Maple Leaf Gardens," Selke said. *"In due course, Verdun met Oshawa in the Eastern Canada Memorial Cup semi-finals. If memory serves me right, Oshawa won the series in three straight games. No one suspected that the hard-driving Richard would some day rewrite the record book.*

"Richard advanced in hockey under conditions that would have cooled off any less dedicated player," Selke added.

"In his rookie year in senior amateur hockey, he suffered a broken ankle and was in forced retirement for the season. The next year he broke his wrist after a few games; again, he watched his teammates from the sidelines. Early in his third season, as a member of the Montreal Canadiens, he fractured his other ankle. I was acting manager of the Toronto Maple Leafs at the time. A few days after his third break, daily newspapers carried a story quoting Tommy Gorman, then the Montreal manager, as saying that Maurice Richard was brittle-boned; his name was being removed from the Canadiens' reserve list.

"It was a chance for all other managers in the NHL to show their acumen by picking up Richard for free – as Detroit did some years later when youthful (Gordie) Howe was cut adrift by New York. None of us were smart enough, however; we all went along with Gorman's analysis.

"But not Dick Irvin, then coaching for Gorman. Dick was cagey enough to think that perhaps the Canadiens had been too hasty in removing the kid's name. He lost no time in saying so. Always a fast mover when he needed to be, Tommy Gorman put Maurice's name back on the Habitant list."

NOVEMBER 3, 1940

The Canadiens and the Bruins tie 1-1 at the Forum in Dick Irvin's first game as Montreal coach.

I still can't figure what Canadiens saw in me to offer me that first pro contract. I was hopelessly awkward and fragile.

– Maurice Richard

^
*Maurice Richard was
genuinely worried about
his resiliency after
injuries side-tracked
his early career.*

The First Major Injury

"Brittle".

"The kid's brittle, he breaks too easily."

"This league may be too tough for him."

With New Year 1943 beckoning, Maurice Richard was in a familiar place, in plaster of Paris, this time for a broken right ankle. Sixteen games and eleven points (five goals and six assists) into his first National Hockey League season, the honeymoon was over. He was out for the year.

The date: December 27, 1942.

With the Canadiens leading the Bruins that night on the strength of a goal and two assists by the rookie, Richard absorbed a hard check from Jack Crawford and fractured his ankle, ironically in the same corner where the great Howie Morenz had suffered his career-ending injury almost six years before

In his first year with Verdun Maple Leafs, Richard had shown much promise until a fractured left ankle ended his season. In senior hockey, he played 20 games and his game improved with each outing until a snapped wrist sidelined him again.

Now, with plaster adorning him once more, the wolves were baying.

In the post-game conference after Richard was injured, Dick Irvin was quoted: *"Richard may just be too brittle to play in the National Hockey League."* Other veterans, Toe Blake prominent among them, concurred.

Even Maurice had his doubts.

"Three major injuries in three years – I wondered, too." Richard recalled. *"I knew I was a lot stronger than they gave me credit for and that I could play against anybody in that league, but I was going to have to prove it. It is hard to fight against the other teams and your own coaches, management and teammates.*

"Getting a reputation that you are injury-prone is something very hard to get rid of. I also knew that if I hurt myself again in the next season or two, the Canadiens might ship me just about anywhere."

A year later, Richard was sidelined early in the season with a dislocated shoulder, but as a full-time member of the Punch Line, he went on to score 32 goals, before exploding in the playoffs with a record dozen goals.

With pucks flying into opposition nets from all over the ice, nobody complained if the Rocket would sit in the dressing room with ice on assorted injuries after the game.

Editors in the Montreal dailies filed away the adjective brittle, never again to be used in conjunction with Maurice Richard.

What Selke wasn't aware of at the time was that Gorman also had offered Richard to the Rangers in a straight swap for fiery Phil Watson. Lester Patrick, the premier hockey executive of the first half of the 20th century, turned down the trade.

Selke's description of Quebec amateur hockey ranks in disarray was a scathing indictment of amateur hockey management in the province, and of a Canadiens hierarchy that had paid little or no attention to nurturing home-grown talent. That helped explain, in part, why so few French-Canadian players emerged with the Habs in the 1930s and early 1940s. This upset Selke's sensibilities. A gentleman farmer who, like Dick Irvin, was a collector of prime poultry, "Farmer Frank" would immediately take charge of minor hockey in Quebec, while investing in teams and entire leagues in the west, when he joined the Canadiens in 1946.

Maurice Richard and his Montreal teammates won Stanley Cups in 1944 and 1946.

The Outdoor Game

Richard and teammates Bob Fillion and Fern Majeau filtered up to the NHL Canadiens because of the work of several indefatigable amateur hockey men; Georges Norchet, Paul-Émile Paquette, Paul Stuart, Arthur Therrien and Paul Haynes, a former NHLer with the Maroons, Bruins and Canadiens.

The eldest son of Onésime and Alice Richard, Gaspesians who had moved to the big city in the post-war (First World War) era, Maurice first skated at age four on a backyard rink built by his father. Onésime was a taciturn and fiercely independent man who worked as a machinist in the Angus Shops of the Canadian Pacific Railway in east-end Montreal. When Maurice was a baby, Onésime and his father-in-law built a home in the distant north-central district of New Bordeaux, as far as one could get from the centre of Montreal at the time.

Organized hockey began at school, as Maurice played peewee, bantam and midget for the teams of St. François-de-Laval school through Grade 9. Having graduated from St. François, the young man enrolled in the Montreal Technical School, played for its hockey team, and also signed up with the Bordeaux district team. He was playing for Bordeaux in midget when he was spotted by Georges Norchet, who immediately passed along the word to his contacts in the Parc Lafontaine juvenile league.

Paul-Émile Paquette was a Montreal businessman who invested the princely sum of $500 a season in a team in the juvenile league. This was the "pros" for the starry-eyed youngsters he signed to play for him. They travelled to games in his Ford panel truck and Réal Bouthier, M.D., a family friend, supplied team medical care gratis.

Paquette and his coach, Paul Stuart, attended a Bordeaux game at Norchet's behest and immediately offered a player contract to Richard. In his first game with his new team, the North Ender scored six goals.

The infant Maurice with parents
Onésime and Alice Richard.

"In 1938-39, our team played 46 games, winning 43, tying two and losing only one," Paquette recalled. "The team scored 144 goals and Maurice scored 133 of these.

"We were in the habit of winning our games 10-0 and 12-0 and Richard was getting eight or 10 goals by himself. We counted on him to provide three-quarters of our offence."

At the time, Richard was playing two games on weeknights and as many as four on weekends, sometimes under an alias. Still, as Frank Selke asserted, the amateur hockey hierarchy in Quebec was in such disarray that junior, senior and professional ranks may have missed Richard altogether had it not been for Stuart.

Paul Stuart, despite his name a francophone, took all thirty-eight teams in the Parc Lafontaine leagues under his wing and undertook to promote the top talents to the city's highest clubs. Stuart realized early on that Richard would be a marked man in the upper echelons of hockey, so he assigned him to top boxing coach Harry Hurst, who discovered that he had a Golden Gloves talent on his hands. Those boxing lessons would serve Richard well in the future.

Stuart, Paquette and Norchet then invited Arthur Therrien, coach of the Verdun Maple Leafs junior team, a farm team of the NHL Canadiens, to watch Richard in action.

Maurice and a teammate pose with benefactor Paul-Émile Paquette.

We were in the habit of winning our games 10-0 and 12-0 and Richard was getting eight or 10 goals by himself. We counted on him to provide three-quarters of our offence.

– Paul-Émile Paquette

Two Solitudes

They had been the *faux Flying Frenchmen* once, trading on the popularity of such stars as the Ontario-bred trio of Newsy Lalonde, Howie Morenz and **Aurel Joliat**.

There had been some homegrown French-Canadian talent, such as Johnny *Black Cat* Gagnon, Battleship Leduc and George Vézina, especially in the days when the Canadiens represented the French East End against the Maroons of the English West End.

But, until the arrival of Maurice Richard, and the subsequent construction of a network of Quebec feeder leagues by Frank Selke, the Flying Frenchmen were the figment of an (American) sports editor's imagination.

The Canadiens were still Montreal's team, but only because there wasn't anything better back then.

In Maurice Richard's case, there was no Hollywood scene where the grizzled bird dog, note pad in hand and fedora pushed back on his head, ticket stubs in the headband, tapped the fresh young talent on the shoulder and pronounced, breathlessly: *"Son, you're going to the Bigs."*

"It never happened that way," Richard said. *"It might have a couple of years later, but the Canadiens didn't have the kind of organization Mr. Selke built. They owned four or five junior teams and controlled senior hockey too, but it was run like a bad orchard. They waited until the wind would blow the apples out of the trees."*

Flying Frenchmen or not, the big club was not about to chase after every talented young French Canadian who came along. In recognition of his organizational talent, Montreal management offered Paul Stuart a coaching and managing position with the Senior Canadiens. When he asked for *carte blanche* to favor French-speaking players, the offer was withdrawn.

Tommy Gorman, an Ottawa native, ran the team for owner Senator Donat Raymond, and he had just reached out to Toronto and hired Dick Irvin, a western Canadian, to coach. Another senior man in the Canadiens hierarchy at the time was Cecil Hart, a well-known West Ender. None of the three had connections in the French or East End hockey community.

French Canadians with names like Norchet, Paquette, Stuart and Therrien paved the way for Maurice Richard. But, they had to be as determined as he was to ensure that he got a fair audition for the Verdun Maple Leaf juniors and, later, the senior and NHL Canadiens.

> ^
> *Newsy Lalonde was the first-ever captain of the Montreal Canadiens.*
>
> *(Above left) The 1930-31 Canadiens won a second consecutive Stanley Cup. They would not win again (1944) until after the arrival of Maurice Richard.*

In September 1939, Richard was one of 126 hopefuls who attended the Leafs camp and, legend has it, earned the twentieth and last spot on the squad. *"You couldn't miss him on the ice,"* said Therrien. *"He wore this ugly yellow sweater with Marvelube (one of the Paquette sponsors) on it. He was only 18 and we had some older, veteran players who were better than him at that point, so he didn't always play a lot at the beginning."*

Still, Richard played enough to earn an invitation to the camp of the senior league Montreal Canadiens the following season, even though he still had a season of junior eligibility remaining.

As Andy O'Brien reported in Rocket Richard: *"Maurice Richard had the fire of greatness within him. But it took a coach, Paul Haynes, to inject a technique without which Maurice Richard would never have strayed off hockey's straight and narrow into the wild, wonderful expanse reserved for the very few who are called."*

The Paquette Midgets, a Parc Lafontaine league powerhouse.
ⅴ

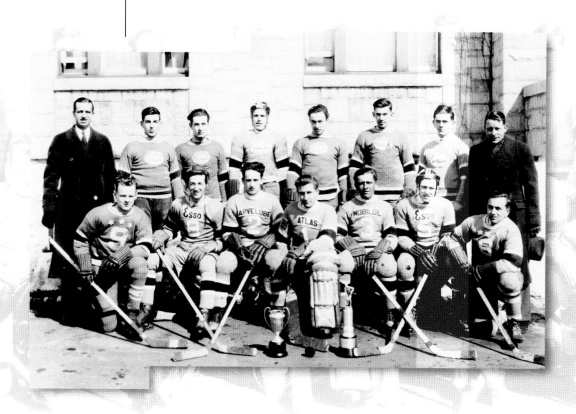

Moving to the 'Right' Side

Every winter saw some 80,000 boys across Canada playing organized hockey. In that era, there were seldom more than 120 players in the NHL, and of those only a handful were newcomers. It was hard to get to the top, harder to stay. In Maurice Richard's case, the key was his being shifted from left wing – his natural side as a left-handed shot – to his wrong wing, the right.

O'Brien added: *"Haynes shifted him because of something he had noticed in practice. 'A left-handed shooter coming in on left wing,' Haynes recently pointed out to me, 'usually has one of two choices if he decides to get in close. One is to try to swing around the left side of the defence, in which case he often gets ridden off a good shooting angle by the defenceman on that side and is forced to keep going around the net or to pass back. The other choice is to veer into the heavily populated area in front of the net, which leaves the puck swinging around in front of him into position for a backhand shot.'*

" 'When, on occasion, he'd find himself way over on the wrong side, he'd button-hook around the other defenceman, using the sheer strength of his left arm, and follow with a burst of speed in between the defenceman and the goal. Normally, that would leave a player a prime target to get reefed in the narrow passage by the first defenceman, now in front of the goal. But so great was the surge of speed that frequently he was out in front before either of the two defencemen or the goalie, realized what was happening. And when Richard pulled the trick, he ended in supreme shooting position as a left-handed shot.' "

September 21, 1942:
Lucille and Maurice
Richard, on the big day.

I Love Lucille

The Maurice Richard who would light up the ice for the Paquette juvenile team, scoring four or five goals a night, was a fading flower indeed when the players would congregate at the Norchet home for post-game or post-practice relaxation.

The dark, shy 17-year-old would stand on the periphery of the action, pensively sipping a soft drink and munching on chips as more gregarious teammates cut a mean rug with some of the young ladies who made a point of attending these regular gatherings.

As much as he tried to fade into the wallpaper, his coach's younger sister, Lucille, who would share her observations with her mother, was noticing him. An effervescent redhead with blue eyes, the 13-year-old homed in on the star player and began to coax some party life into him.

"Maurice had no girlfriend, and he lived the farthest away from Parc Lafontaine, way out in New Bordeaux, and I believe some nights he didn't have a lift home so he'd stay with us," Lucille reminisced.

"We would roll up the rugs and dance and I took it upon myself to teach Maurice to dance, and to act as his fashion consultant, too," she laughed.

"He used to wear his hair fairly long and comb it straight back off his forehead. I told him a part on the side would look better, and he did it and that's how he wore his hair for the rest of his life. I taught him how to dance; his favorite was the rumba."

While Lucille's parents closely chaperoned events, they were astonished when a 20-year-old Richard, now with the senior Canadiens and making $20 a week as a machinist, asked for 17-year-old Lucille's hand. Onésime and Alice Richard were also taken aback, but all agreed that this was a serious young couple that was proposing a lifetime together. Reluctantly, they acquiesced.

On September 21, 1942, Maurice Richard, just turned 21, married Lucille Norchet. Two weeks later, his honeymoon with the Montreal Canadiens of the National Hockey League began.

Maurice and Lucille would be together for 52 years, until she passed away of cancer in 1994. Model parents, they raised seven children.

The relationship with the Canadiens would last even longer.

^
Paul Haynes made Maurice's career with a simple suggestion: switch sides.

No less a hockey mind than Frank Selke gave Paul Haynes full credit for the Richard switch-over, saying he was following in the skate tracks of successful NHL players Cecil Dillon and Bryan Hextall.

"Both these boys, like Maurice, were left-handed shots. If a player is handy enough to play what hockey men call his wrong wing, he does have quite an edge over his more orthodox rivals. To begin with, it gives him a lot more net to shoot at; it also forces him to develop a backhand shot, which if accurate, is the bane of all goalkeepers. Helge Bostrum, Busher Jackson, Bryan Hextall, and Maurice Richard had the most devastating backhands of my experience. It is a fast, rapidly rising shot that seems to be almost non-existent in today's game."

When Richard showed up at his first NHL training camp, he was one of many Quebec-bred forwards trying to win a spot on the team. It became evident early on in the proceedings that he had the offensive talent to help a Montreal team singularly lacking in that area. Dick Irvin and some of his veteran talents were leaning against the boards near the team bench when the question of Richard's toughness arose. It was agreed that hard rock forward Murph Chamberlain would test the rookie's mettle.

NOVEMBER 8, 1942

Maurice and his buddy Elmer test some early cranial protection. Despite their early testing, helmets would not become a standard piece of equipment until the 1970s.

Chamberlain obliged by running Richard into the boards with a resounding thump. The rookie went down, sprang to his feet and went straight for his tormenter. It took three teammates to extricate Chamberlain from Richard's inflamed clutches. Question asked, and answered.

Joseph Henri Maurice Richard signed his first NHL contract as a left-winger. Fifty-six seconds into his first game on Halloween night, he and line-mate Elmer Lach set up right-winger Tony Demers for a goal, en route to a 3-2 win over the Bruins.

Jacques Plante, who joined the team a decade after Richard, tells of the Rocket's earliest beginnings, recounting an apocryphal story which would be used to prove a point to all Habs' rookies down through the years.

"When Rocket first came up in 1942, to show you what kind of guy he was, he was a rookie at the same time as Bobby Fillion of Thetford Mines. Dick Irvin... played them off against each other. Both players would skate in the pre-game warm-up, but they didn't know until after the warm-up which one would be playing. After it was over Irvin would tell them who was playing and who

would have to get undressed. One day Rocket was told to go to the room and he just kicked the door right through, he put his foot right through the door and went in to have his shower. He was twenty-one years old, a rookie, and to do that to Dick Irvin showed that he had a lot of character. This was the type of guy Irvin was looking for. Irvin would love a good fight on the ice during practice. He would instigate things, people would blow off steam, and then laugh about it afterwards."

Maurice Richard entered through the side door, and kicked down a few more, but within two NHL seasons the entire hockey world would recognize the man with the blazing eyes who routinely carried a pair of opponents on his back while scoring prodigious goals.

He was twenty-one years old, a rookie, and to do that to Dick Irvin showed that he had a lot of character.

– Jacques Plante

The First Game

^
*Maurice would pose
many times with pucks
in his career.*

A very special "Forum ghost" was in the house on Halloween night, 1942, as the Canadiens and Boston launched the new season.

Aurel Joliat, former all-star winger alongside Howie Morenz and Johnny *Black Cat* Gagnon in the team's halcyon days, had just joined the National Hockey League as a linesman. Little did Joliat know that his return to the Forum ice would coincide with the launch of the career of the man who would, finally, replace the Stratford Streak, Morenz, in the hearts of Hab fans everywhere.

Starting on left wing that night, alongside centre Elmer Lach and right-winger Tony Demers was Maurice Richard, a swarthy and well-built winger who had spent two injury-plagued seasons with the Canadiens' senior league team. Glen Harmon and Leo Lamoureux were newcomers to the Montreal defence, and veterans Gord Drillon and Dutch Hiller had been acquired from Toronto and Boston respectively to add punch to what had been an anemic offence. Drillon was the prize, a sniper whose twenty-three goals and eighteen assists left him tied for seventh in the NHL scoring race the previous season, just four points behind Montreal leader Toe Blake.

The Bruins, fully aware of the potency of the Blake-Drillon combination, checked them relentlessly, allowing the Lach-Demers-Richard trio more leeway. This oversight cost them the game, 3-2, with Demers scoring a pair of goals and the rookie Richard chipping in one assist.

A little more than a week later, the Canadiens came up against a very special character. Steve Buzinski had learned the art of the wisecrack early in his abbreviated National Hockey League career. Or maybe it was the rubber bombardment that he was subjected to each night his wartime-depleted New York Rangers took to the ice against other NHL squads that had vulcanized his brain.

Manhattan writers who were subjected to his Madison Square Garden performances that season often called him Steve (The Puck Goes Inski) Buzinski.

With Dave Kerr retired in 1941, his replacement Sugar Jim Henry and recently acquired Chuck Rayner both in military service in the fall of 1942, the Rangers plucked Buzinski out of the ranks of intermediate hockey in Swift Current, Saskatchewan, to anchor a netminding triad that included journeymen Bill Beveridge and Jimmy Franks. In all, he would see action in nine games, giving up 55 goals, before the Broadway Blueshirts, mercifully, ended his misery.

On November 8, Buzzer visited the Forum with his Ranger mates, proud winners of a 4-3 game over the Canadiens the night before. It was a tainted triumph, however. Newly introduced wartime travel restrictions, necessitated special travelling passes or visas for all players crossing the border to play league games. Several Canadiens, including rookie forward Maurice Richard, could not get their paperwork processed in time and remained in Montreal.

The full-squad Canadiens were waiting for the Rangers for the return contest, and it was **Steve Buzinski** who paid dearly in a 10-4 rout.

Early in the second period, a young Montreal left winger picked up the puck behind goalie Paul Bibeault's net and headed up ice. The dark-haired rookie in the No. 15 sweater skated through the entire New York team, finishing off the play with a "top shelf" backhander that had a chagrined Buzinski fishing the puck out of the net while the Forum faithful responded with the first of a lifetime of standing ovations.

He wasn't the Rocket just yet, but Maurice Richard had scored his first NHL goal. And the Buzzer was in the history books.

A SUPERSTAR IS BORN

*T*he ineffable Conn Smythe, majority owner

and managing partner of the Toronto Maple

Leafs discovered the phenomenon that was

Maurice *Rocket* Richard late in the piece. He

had a valid excuse. From 1943 to 1945, he was

overseas with the Thirtieth Battery, Royal Canadian

Artillery, as well as in military hospital recovering

from war wounds, and his right-hand man, Frank Selke,

was minding the store on Carlton Street. **9**

We leave it to the No. 1 Maple Leaf to mark, officially, the ascension of Maurice Richard to NHL superstardom.

"All this time I hadn't seen a hockey game," Smythe said. *"I listened to Foster Hewitt on the radio, of course, but I wasn't that well and the cold really got to me... I'd been running the hockey side of the Gardens by telephone from my bedside. But I wasn't ready to watch a game until the night of my fiftieth birthday, February 1, 1945, when Chicago had a game scheduled in Montreal and an NHL Governors' meeting would be held the next day. I decided to make that trip to Montreal my big return. Selke had been telling me how terrible wartime hockey was. I had never seen Rocket Richard before, but I saw a lot of him that night. It was a 1-1 tie and Rocket got the Montreal goal. He went in from the blue line with a big defenceman draped all over him on one side and Johnny Gottselig draped all over him on the other. Still, the Rocket walked in, pulled the goalkeeper, and put the puck in the net. I demanded of Selke: 'What kind of lies have you been telling me? That's as good a hockey play as I ever saw in my whole life.'*

Richard scores on Turk Broda.

"I offered Montreal $25,000 for Richard, which they were smart enough to turn down."

Smythe and Richard would enjoy a curious love-hate relationship over the years.

"In Toronto, I had a box just in front of the greens and would be in the thick of things often enough," Smythe said. "The night of the famous fight between Rocket Richard and Bob Bailey, a real wild one, I went to the press room after that and when a reporter asked me what I thought, I said: 'We've got to stamp out that kind of thing, or people are going to keep on buying tickets.' You should have heard the editorial writers baying at the moon over that one, which later made the rounds in Sports Illustrated *and even the* Encyclopedia Britannica.

SUMMER PURSUITS

The Canadiens got together every summer to play in baseball and softball charity events.

"One night there was practically a riot at the Gardens. Rocket Richard was in that one, too. After he had been sent to the dressing room by the referee I was down in the corridor. Suddenly the door flew open and he charged out again. His eyes blazing the way he sometimes got, in what somebody once called the Rocket's red glare, so mad he was not seeing anything. I stepped in front of him and said: 'Rocket! Where are you going! Won't do you any good! Get back!'

That's as good a hockey play as
I ever saw in my whole life.

– Conn Smythe

50 in 50

When Rocket Richard scored 50 goals in the 50 games of the 1944-45 season, it was the first noteworthy feat of his extraordinary career. But it remains a controversial one, its merits still debated 55 years later.

The Second World War was in its final year and many top NHL players were in the Canadian military. Thus, the view of some was that Richard scored his goal-a-game in a watered-down league.

Richard himself was not in the service because, in three seasons from 1940 to '43, he had suffered two broken ankles and a broken wrist. But in an unusual twist, several players who failed physicals for the military, played in the NHL.

Three top goalies, Frank Brimsek (Boston), Turk Broda (Toronto) and Chuck Rayner (New York) were not in the league. But Richard's favorite target that season (14 goals, five in one game), Harry Lumley of the Detroit Red Wings, was starting a Hall of Fame career, Chicago's Mike Karakas played 336 NHL games, and Frank McCool, who backed the Toronto Maple Leafs to the 1945 Stanley Cup, was a high-quality NHL goalie who retired early because of stomach ulcers.

With 32 goals, plus 12 playoff scores in the 1943-44 season, the Rocket provided a preview of what was to come in his career. The following year, working with Punch Line mates, centre Elmer Lach and left-winger Toe Blake, Richard scored goals in 34 of the 50 games. He had a five-goal game, three games with three goals and two goals in six games. The Rocket scored 32 goals at home, 18 on the road.

Richard's fiftieth goal in the fiftieth game of the season, of course, created a debate. In the season finale at Boston, rookie back-up Harvey Bennett, who took over for Paul Bibeault halfway through the game, held off Richard until 17:45 of the third period.

Because no film or video was made of the game as it is now to settle most disputes, assorted descriptions of the goal were delivered. At the time, Bennett protested to the officials that the puck was kicked in. Another version had Lach bumping into Bennett allowing Richard to knock the puck into the net.

Looking back, Bennett refuses to be drawn into the controversy, claiming that Richard was the best player in history.

Rangers coach Frank Boucher's first impression of Richard was that he would be a "wartime wonder." A few years later, Boucher admitted his assessment was wrong and that Richard was *"the most spectacular player I have ever seen, and that includes Howie Morenz."*

	Game		Result	Goalie	G	Assists	Game			Year Total		
							G	A	Pts	G	A	Pts
1	Oct. 28	Boston	W 3-2	H. Bennett	0		0	0	0	0	0	0
2	Nov. 2	Toronto	L 4-1	F. McCool	0		0	0	0	0	0	0
3	Nov. 4	Detroit	W 3-2	C. Dion	1	Lach	1	0	1	1	0	1
4	Nov. 5	Detroit	W 3-2	C.Dion	0		0	0	0	1	0	1
5	Nov. 9	Chicago	W 9-2	M. Karakas	3	Blake, Lach	3	2	5	4	2	6
					–	Blake, Lach						
					–	Blake						
6	Nov. 11	Toronto	L 3-1	F. McCool	0		0	0	0	4	2	6
7	Nov. 12	Chicago	W 4-2	M. Karakas	1	Lach	1	0	1	5	2	7
8	Nov. 18	Boston	W 6-3	H. Bennett	1	Blake, Lach	1	0	1	6	2	8
9	Nov. 19	Rangers	W 6-2	K. McAuley	1	Blake, Lamoureux	1	1	2	7	3	10
10	Nov. 21	Boston	W 4-1	H. Bennett	1	Blake	1	0	1	8	3	11
11	Nov. 23	Detroit	T 3-3	C. Dion	1	Blake, Bouchard	1	0	1	9	3	12
12	Nov. 25	Toronto	L 2-0	F. McCool	0		0	0	0	9	3	12
13	Nov. 26	Toronto	W 4-1	F. McCool	3	Blake, Lach	3	0	3	12	3	15
						Blake, Lach						
						Blake, Eddolis						
14	Nov. 30	Rangers	L 7-5	K. McAuley	1	Blake, Lach	1	1	2	13	4	17
15	Dec. 3	Chicago	W 2-1	M Karakas	1	Lach	1	0	1	14	4	18
16	Dec. 5	Boston	W 4-1	H. Bennett	2	Blake	1	1	2	15	5	20
17	Dec 14	Toronto	T 2-2	F. McCool	1	Blake, Bouchard	1	0	1	16	5	21
18	Dec. 16	Boston	W 8-5	H. Bennett	2	Blake, Lach	2	1	3	18	6	24
					–	Blake, Lach						
19	Dec. 17	Rangers	W 4-1	K. McAuley	1	Lach, O'Connor	1	0	1	19	6	25
20	Dec. 23	Chicago	W 2-1	M. Karakas	0		0	0	0	19	6	25
21	Dec. 28	Detroit	W 9-1	H. Lumley	5	Lamoureux	5	3	8	24	9	33
					–	Lach						
					–	Blake, Lach						
					–	Eddolls, Lach						
22	Dec. 30	Rangers	W 4-1	K. McAuley	0		0	1	1	24	10	34
23	Jan. 2	Boston	W 6-3	P. Bibeault	1	Blake, Lach	1	1	2	25	11	36
24	Jan. 4	Toronto	L 4-2	F. McCool	0		0	0	0	25	11	36
25	Jan. 6	Chicago	W 10-1	M. Karakas	1	Lach, Harmon	1	2	3	26	13	39
26	Jan. 11	Toronto	W 7-4	F. McCool	2	Bouchard	2	1	3	28	14	42
						Blake, Lach						
27	Jan. 13	Detroit	W 8-3	H. Lumley	1		1	0	1	29	14	43
28	Jan. 14	Rangers	W 6-2	K. McAuley	0		0	1	1	29	15	44
29	Jan. 17	Chicago	W 4-2	M. Karakas	0		0	0	0	29	15	44
30	Jan. 20	Rangers	W 5-2	K. McKauley	1		1	1	2	30	16	46
31	Jan. 21	Detroit	W 6-3	H. Lumley	3		3	0	3	33	16	49
					–	Lach						
					–	O'Connor						
32	Jan. 27	Boston	W 11-3	P. Bibeault	1	Blake, Lach	1	2	3	34	18	52
33	Jan. 28	Boston	W 4-1	P. Bibeault	2	Lach	2	0	2	36	18	54
						Blake						
34	Feb. 1	Chicago	T 1-1	M. Karakas	1	Lach, Bouchard	1	0	1	37	18	55
35	Feb. 3	Detroit	W 5-2	H. Lumley	1		1	1	2	38	19	57
36	Feb. 4	Detroit	W 3-1	H. Lumley	1		1	0	1	39	19	58
37	Feb. 8	Rangers	W 9-4	K. McAuley	2	Lamoureux	2	0	2	41	19	60
					–	Blake						
38	Feb. 10	Detroit	W 5-2	H. Lumley	2	Lach	2	0	2	43	19	62
					–	Blake						
39	Feb. 11	Rangers	W 4-3	D. Stevenson	0		0	2	2	43	21	64
40	Feb. 17	Toronto	W 4-3	F. McCool	1	Lach	1	0	1	44	21	65
41	Feb. 18	Chicago	T 0-0	M. Karakas	0		0	0	0	44	21	65
42	Feb. 25	Toronto	W 5-2	F. McCool	1	Blake	1	0	1	45	21	66
43	Mar. 3	Toronto	L 3-2	F. McCool	0		0	1	1	45	22	67
44	Mar. 4	Chicago	L 6-4	M. Karakas	1	Blake, Lamoureux	1	0	1	46	22	68
45	Mar. 8	Boston	W 3-2	P. Bibeault	0		0	0	0	46	22	68
46	Mar. 10	Rangers	W 7-3	K. McAuley	0		0	0	0	46	22	68
47	Mar. 11	Rangers	W 11-5	K. McAuley	2	Lach	2	0	2	48	22	70
					–	Blake						
48	Mar. 15	Detroit	L 2-1	H. Lumley	1	Lach	1	0	1	49	22	71
49	Mar. 17	Chicago	W 4-3	D. Stevenson	0		0	0	0	49	22	71
50	Mar. 18	Boston	W 4-2	H. Bennett	1	Lach	1	1	2	50	23	73

SEASON 1944-45

© The Hockey News

"He seemed to come to. He stared at me. Then, without a word, he stomped back into the dressing room. I admired that man tremendously, would have given anything to have him play for me, but that didn't stop me from giving it to him when he was the enemy. Once in Montreal, I asked for seats where I wouldn't get into trouble and some joker, no doubt Selke, put me beside the Rocket's mother-in-law. We fought all through the game. Finally, we were yelling at each other. When it died down a little I asked her what she had been saying in French. She told me, and then said: 'That's where I have it on you, Mr. Smitty. I can tell you what I think of you in both languages.' "

Referee Red Storey remembered the Bob Bailey incident, and Smythe's reaction, as well.

"After we got peace restored, I threw him (Richard) out of the game and an ugly mob of really angry fans was lying in wait for him. Conn Smythe, who ran the Maple Leafs and had no time for the Canadiens in general, came rushing over and I thought: 'Oh, oh, here we go.' But what Smythe did was urge the police to 'protect that man. He's the greatest hockey player in the world.' "

A Superstar is Born

33

Frank Selke acknowledges Smythe's special feeling for Richard.

"Conn Smythe was quick to appreciate the Rocket's potential as a hockey star," Selke said. *"One night in the directors' room at the Forum during the intermission period of a hockey game, Conn – who had earlier that week been quoted as saying Richard was a top scorer but a player who couldn't backcheck – offered Senator Donat Raymond, then president of the Canadiens, $75,000 for Richard's playing contract.*

"The Senator, who loved to beat Toronto more than anything else in life, answered: 'I have read that you say Richard won't backcheck. You say he is only a great player when he is advancing. Does this mean that, if I get him to play coming and going, you would offer me $150,000?'"

"Two years later, Happy Day, coaching the Maple Leafs, wired me to this effect: 'I have been authorized by my superiors to offer you $135,000 for Maurice Richard's playing contract,'" Selke said. *"Without consulting a soul, I wired back: 'Quit cracking jokes. If I disposed of Richard, the whole team would be chased out of town by our aroused fans. (Signed) Frank J. Selke.' In all of his years of playing, there was never any money that could buy the Rocket."*

Maurice and Elmer Lach on father-and-son day at the Forum, with Frank Selke.
∨

In all of his years of playing, there was
never any money that could buy the Rocket.

– Frank J. Selke

Number Nine for Montreal Canadiens

On October 30, 1943, Maurice Richard officially took possession of the Montreal Canadiens' jersey bearing the No. 9. Whereas his predecessors had "rented," the sweater, the Rocket would claim ownership in perpetuity.

For trivia buffs, Maurice Richard is only one of three Hall of Fame hockey players to wear that number for Montreal.

He wasn't even the fiercest competitor to sport No. 9 for the Canadiens. That distinction falls to William (Bill) Coutu, a robust defenceman, who after being traded to Boston, was suspended for life by NHL President Frank Calder.

The incident that led to Coutu's (sometimes known as Couture) demise, took place in Ottawa on April 11, 1927, after the Senators had defeated Boston 2-0 to win the Stanley Cup. Enraged by several calls and incidents in what had been a vicious game, Coutu attacked referee Jerry Laflamme in the corridor leading to the dressing rooms. When Laflamme's officiating partner Billy Bell jumped into the fray, Coutu attacked him too.

Irony of ironies, Bell had been the next player to wear number No. 9 with the Canadiens after Coutu debuted the number in his first stint with the Habs in 1918-20. Bell wore it as a "call-up" in 1922-23 (he also later wore number 11). Coutu's lifetime ban was later rescinded, but he never played another game in the National Hockey League.

Sylvio Mantha, captain of the team in two segments, 1926-32 and 1933-36, was more familiar to Montreal fans in shirts bearing numbers two and three, but wore No. 9 in his rookie season of 1923-24. He would be elected to the Hall of Fame in September, 1960.

Journeyman Jean Matz wore sweater No. 9 for 35 games in 1924-25, before Alfred *Pit* Lépine appropriated it in 1926, and kept it for a dozen seasons. Lépine was the second-highest Canadiens scorer in that jersey, with 141 goals and 104 assists in regular season and playoffs. He later went on to coach Montreal after Babe Siebert drowned in a summer accident.

When the Maroons were dissolved after the 1938 season, the Canadiens picked up veteran winger Herb Cain and he wore No. 9 for the 1938-39 season, before being traded to Boston. He would play seven years in Beantown, ironically winning the NHL scoring championship in 1943-44 with 36 goals and 46 assists for 82 points, stealing a bit of thunder away from a rookie named Richard who scored 32 goals while wearing No. 9 for the first time.

Veteran Marty Barry, who had led Detroit to a pair of Stanley Cups in the mid-1930s, was on his last legs in 1939-40 when he was traded to the Habs to take a curtain call in his hometown. Barry scored four goals and 10 assists in his final 30 games in the league, and was inducted into the Hockey Hall of Fame in June of 1965.

The penultimate bearer of the Canadiens number nine? Right-winger Charlie Sands, 1940-43, the man whom Maurice Richard replaced on a line with Elmer Lach and Toe Blake.

Five Against the Leafs

After Dick Irvin fortuitously created the offensively prolific Punch Line, Maurice Richard's career took off. Richard enjoyed a 32-goal season, adding 22 assists for 54 points, and the Canadiens turned in the best season in league history, winning 38 games, losing five and tying seven to run away with the regular-season title, finishing an unprecedented 25 points (83) ahead of runner-up Detroit (58).

In the 1944 Stanley Cup playoff semi-final, the Canadiens met the Maple Leafs, who were regarded as an easy foe, 33 points inferior during the season.

Backed by the brilliant goaltending of ex-Hab Paul Bibeault, the Leafs stunned The Forum with a 3-1 win. Bibeault turned aside 60 shots, while the Leafs scored on three of 23. Richard told his boyhood friend between games: *"You were too hot for us in the first game, Paul, but I'll give you something to think about in the next one."* He was prophetic.

Defensive winger Bob Davidson was assigned to Richard, containing the Rocket in the scoreless first period of game two, on March 23.

His luck ran out in the second period. Early in the period, Richard and Davidson were locked in a loveless embrace in the corner of the Toronto zone, the puck skittering at their feet. Davidson later said that he had Richard pinned to the boards, when a Montreal fan reached out and *"grabbed my stick... yanked it right out of my hands."* While Davidson waited for a whistle that never came, Rocket gathered in the puck and walked in on Bibeault and scored.

Seventeen seconds later, Richard made it 2-0. Richard was even involved in Toronto's only goal of the contest, sitting out a penalty when Reg Hamilton scored at 8:50. After serving his second minor penalty of the period, the Rocket scored his third goal at 16:46 and the issue was no longer in doubt.

That didn't stop him, however. With Elwyn Morris serving a Toronto penalty to start the third period, Richard scored during the Canadiens' only power play of the game, and sealed the issue with a final goal at 8:54 of the final period. Toe Blake matched his linemate with five points, all on assists, while Elmer Lach added four helpers.

Elmer Ferguson of the *Montreal Herald* picked the three stars, and instantaneously became the most despised journalist in the building when the P.A. announcer intoned, *"Tonight's Third Star... Maurice Richard!"* Shock and scattered boos greeted the announcement.

"And now, tonight's Second Star... Maurice Richard!" The brighter lights in the house got out, Ferguson was restored to popularity, and the applause began to build.

The announcer barely got the words to *"Tonight's First Star... Maurice Richard!"* before the Forum was engulfed in cataclysmic cheering.

Game Summary

First Period

No scoring
Penalties – Lamoureux, Mtl 6:43

Second Period

1. Mtl Richard (Blake, McMahon) 1:48
2. Mtl Richard (Blake, Lach) 2:05
3. Tor Hamilton (Carr, Morris) pp 8:50
4. Mtl Richard (Lach, Blake) 16:46
Penalties – Richard Mtl 8:34, Richard Mtl, Webster Tor 12:20, Morris Tor 19:24

Third Period

5. Mtl Richard (Blake, Lach) pp 1:00
6. Mtl Richard (Blake, Lach) 8:54
Penalties – Heffernan Mtl 14:57
Powerplay conversions
Toronto 1/3; Montreal 1/1

Enter the Punch Line

How did Maurice Richard go from a brittle player on a waiver wire to the NHL's pre-eminent superstar in such a short period of time?

Dick Irvin deserves the credit, teaming Richard with veterans Toe Blake and Elmer Lach in training camp that fall. Charlie Sands, a right-winger who had played with Blake for most of the previous season, had been sent to New York with Dutch Hiller in a wartime deal that brought Phil Watson to Montreal. Another right-winger, Gord Drillon, who had scored twenty-eight goals the previous season on a line with Buddy O'Connor and Ray Getliffe, joined the Royal Canadian Air Force and would officially retire from hockey at war's end. Also new to the team that September was goalie Bill Durnan, replacing Paul Bibeault.

Irvin recalled Paul Haynes's recommendation from amateur hockey and switched Richard over to the right wing, with Blake and Lach. Within two practices, the genius of the move had become apparent to all.

"You couldn't get the puck from them in practice," said Getliffe, whose line often came up against the new trio.

"They had a lot of skill, and personal abilities that complemented each other. All three of them were as tough as nails, and could play any kind of hockey you wanted – finesse, speed or back alley."

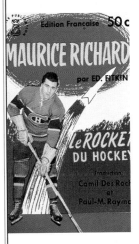

The Rocket is Launched

The Rocket!

No athlete's nickname was better suited to the man and his style. The Babe, for George Herman Ruth, was perhaps the only handle in the class of "the Rocket" for Joseph Henri Maurice Richard.

"The best nickname ever for an athlete for two reasons," said goalie Jacques Plante. *"First, there was the way Maurice would turn on his rockets from the blue line to the net. Then, there was his eyes, as bright as the glare from any rocket. How many times did you read or hear that phrase from The Star Spangled Banner 'and the rocket's red glare' or a play on it, used about Richard?"*

Like many things about Richard and his career, there is no unanimous agreement on where the nickname, the Rocket, originated. In his first season, one of two French-language reporters called him the Comet, but it failed to stick.

One source often mentioned is Harold Atkins, a writer for the *Montreal Star* who later was that paper's sports editor for many years. Most observers of the era attribute the creation of the sobriquet to teammate Ray Getliffe.

Reflecting on Richard's passing in June 2000, Getliffe, a good two-way NHL forward for three seasons with the Boston Bruins and six with the Canadiens, recalled the first time he used the word "rocket" to describe Richard.

"I'm not sure, but I think the name came up in his second year (1943-44)," Getliffe, 86, told sports columnist Jim Kernaghan of *The Free Press* in London, Ont., where the former player has lived for many years.

"I was on the bench when he (Richard) got the puck at the blue line, deked two guys and streaked in with that fire in his eyes to score. I said: 'Jeez, he went in like a rocket'.

"Dink Carroll (a sports writer for The Gazette*) was standing behind the bench and that's when he publicly became Rocket Richard. I guess it's one of the most famous names in sports."*

Scoring in Bunches

With apologies to the people who produce Heritage Moments for television, the Rocket's "legend was born" long before the night when he scored five goals and three assists against Detroit... after spending the day moving house.

As the TV script would have it, Maurice Richard was given a night off on Saturday, December 28, 1944, because he planned to haul furniture that day, and then received a telephone call in mid-move informing him he had to play, before dragging his weary bones to the Forum where he exploded in a 9-1 victory.

Needless to say, no healthy NHL player in the 1940s would receive permission to sit out a game, especially for something as mundane as moving house. Moreover, the Canadiens and Red Wings were fighting tooth-and-nail for first place in the league standings. As for a legend a-birthing, the Christmas week outburst in 1944 was only the Rocket's eighth hat trick-plus in 363 days. That's right... eight games of three-or-more goals in less than a calendar year. The National Hockey League had never seen anything like it.

In his career, the Rocket would score three goals or more in a game 26 times in regular-season play, and another seven times in Stanley Cup competition.

The woeful Blackhawks were his favorite prey, giving up 11 multiple-goal games to the Rocket, one in play-offs, but Toronto and Detroit were right behind, with seven and six hats conceded, respectively.

The stingiest team when it came to limiting multiple-goal Rocket launches was Boston. The Bruins were stung only twice, on Feb. 3, 1951, as he turned in three goals and an assist in a 4-1 Forum win, and on April 14, 1953, when his hat trick sparked a 7-3 win at Boston Garden, and a 3-1 Montreal lead in their best-of-seven semi-final. The Rangers were victims a total of five times, once in playoff action.

How important was Maurice Richard's prolific scoring to his team? In the 26 "hat trick" games, the Canadiens won 24, tied one and lost one. In the seven playoff match-ups, they won them all. In five of the 33 games, he scored all of his team's goals.

A legend was born?

Indeed.

Hats Off to Maurice

December 30, 1943

Maurice Richard scores his first NHL hat trick and adds two assists in an 8-3 Forum shellacking of the Red Wings

February 17, 1944

Richard scores three goals in a stretch of 2:13 to lead the Canadiens to a 3-2 win over the Red Wings in Detroit

March 5, 1944

Montreal beats Toronto 8-3 at the Forum; the Rocket has three goals and an assist

March 23, 1944

The Rocket scores all five of his team's goals as the Canadiens win game two of their semi-final, 5-1, at the Forum (playoffs)

April 4, 1944

The Rocket scores all three of his team's goals as the Canadiens defeat Chicago 3-1 in game two of the Stanley Cup final, at the Forum (playoffs)

November 9, 1944

The Rocket turns in his fourth career regular-season "hat" with three goals and a pair of assists, in a 9-2 win over the visiting Blackhawks

November 26, 1944

Richard has three more goals in a 4-1 win over the visiting Leafs

December 28, 1944

The Rocket moves furniture, and then pots five goals and three assists in a 9-1 Forum win over the Red Wings

Strangely enough, it took the new trio almost half a season to get going, partially because of shoulder injuries to Richard and Blake. The Punch Line, as the trio was called, began to emerge from the shadows in the season's third month and Blake was the game's first star when he returned from his shoulder injury on December 19, leading the Canadiens over Boston, 3-1. On December 30, Richard turned in his first career hat trick, and added a pair of assists, in an 8-3 dismantling of the visiting Red Wings. The Punch Line, ably backed up by trios pivoted by Buddy O'Connor and Phil Watson, steamrolled the league from that point on. When the Canadiens lost 5-0 at Maple Leaf Gardens on January 11, the defeat snapped a nine-game winning skein.

You couldn't get the puck from them in practice.

– Ray Getliffe

SEASON 1946-47

Toe Blake and his very expensive caddy on the links. Although the Rocket was a proficient golfer, his abiding love of fishing kept his handicap in the low teens.

It proved the proverbial bump in the road. Montreal was 11 points ahead of the Leafs after that loss, on a record of 20-3-3 for 43 points (Toronto 15-11-2 for 32 points). The Canadiens would lose only two more games that season, winning 18 more and tying seven games to finish 25 points better than runner-up Detroit.

The newly baptized Rocket scored his second hat trick of the season on February 17, potting all of his team's goals in a 3-2 victory over Toronto. Nine days later, and with nine games remaining in the season, Montreal routed Boston 10-2 and clinched the league championship.

The Punch Line stamped their logo on the playoffs, as Blake, Richard and Lach scored 18, 17 and 13 points respectively to finish 1-2-3 in post-season scoring. The Canadiens won their first Stanley Cup in 13 years in nine games, one over the limit, reeling off eight straight after dropping the first game of the semi-final against Toronto. Richard scored a record 12 goals in that period.

Selke remembered the Punch Line from his Toronto days.

"One hockey writer compared this threesome to a 'trio of mad dogs in their savage quest for goals,'" Selke said. *"I remember coming down with (coach) Hap Day and the Maple Leafs to play league games where this same Punch Line kept us bottled up behind the blue line by their sheer sustained ferocity."*

One thing was certain. The Rocket had arrived, and the league was in for a terrific ride over the next 16 seasons.

FARMER FRANK'S
RECONSTRUCTION

*T*he Montreal Canadiens had come a long

way in the mid-1940s under the stewardship of

Senator Donat Raymond and general manager

Tommy Gorman. Still, the Senator was well aware

that the team would flounder without a talent

pipeline similar to that operating in Ontario for the

Toronto Maple Leafs. The architect of that system

was not Conn Smythe; rather it was his right-hand

man, Frank Selke. If Maurice Richard truly bloomed as

the superstar of his era, it is because a diminutive manager

from Kitchener in the heartland of Ontario found his way

to Montreal. ❾

Farmer Frank was an electrician by trade, chief electrician of the University of Toronto and the man in charge of the school's hockey program when Smythe enticed him into the professional ranks with the Leafs. Selke set about building a Marlboros-St. Michael's College farm system that would feature some of the best young talent in Ontario, as well as the rest of Canada.

When he joined the team, Selke brought with him the explosive Kid Line of Joe Primeau, Charlie Conacher and Harvey *Busher* Jackson, as well as defenceman Red Horner, all players nurtured in his Marlboros' program. Toronto immediately reaped the benefits with a Stanley Cup, and Selke was Smythe's top hockey executive for a decade and a half.

Fortunately for the Canadiens, Conn Smythe had the largest ego in the National Hockey League, and when the Selke-led Leafs managed to snare a Cup in 1945 with Smythe in the military, something had to give. Upon Smythe's return, he fabricated a palace revolt, accused Selke of disloyalty, and the latter was out of the organization. When his former employee found his way to Montreal, Smythe was beside himself.

MARCH 5, 1949

A prime ministerial greeting for the Rocket from a big fan, Canadian PM Louis St. Laurent.

The Stanley Cup champions visit Montreal City Hall in April, 1946.
ˇ

Selke joined Montreal on August 1, 1946, scant months after the Canadiens' second Cup in three years, and immediately set to work at improving the team. Some hockey historians have postulated that Selke's predecessor, Tommy Gorman, was treated shabbily by Senator Raymond, considering that his team won two Cups in three years and should have had three in a row. However, the reality was that the Canadiens were an aging, veteran-laden club that almost had not discovered Maurice Richard.

The general manager's son, Frank Selke Jr., discussed the situation with the coach's son, Dick Irvin Jr., in the latter's book, *The Habs*.

"When my father came to Montreal, junior hockey was almost non-existent," Selke Jr. said. *"My recollection is that the junior teams played late at night, very often in the Forum after the NHL game. There was nobody in the building to watch, nobody seemed to care.*

There was nobody in the building
to watch, nobody seemed to care.

– Frank Selke Jr.

The Goalies

Walter *Turk* Broda was the rotund goalie for the Toronto Maple Leafs, the NHL's best team in the late 1940s, winners of the Stanley Cup in four of five seasons from 1947 to 1951. Twice, the Leafs beat the Montreal Canadiens in the final, which meant their defence and Broda were effective in controlling Maurice Richard.

"Best way of stopping the Rocket? Prayer!" **Broda** said, reflecting on his career. *"Richard was the toughest to stop because he never knew what he was going to do himself, so how could a goalie figure him out?*

"I bet in his entire career he never once said that if he was in alone on a particular goalie, he would use this move or that. He just did it on reflex, taking whatever was available. On one rush, he would use the defenceman as a screen and shoot a hard forehand. The next rush might be an identical play but he would try to cut around the defenceman and flip a backhander when the goalie pulled off the post."

The Rocket was one of a kind to Emile *The Cat* Francis, who logged NHL time with Chicago and New York.

"From the blue line in, I never saw a player as exciting as Richard," Francis said. *"When he had the goalie beat, he finished it off, and you had no chance to recover.*

"When I was with the Blackhawks, he made the greatest play I've ever seen. Richard came in from the blue line, two big defencemen, Bill Gadsby and Ralph Nattrass, were hanging on him all the way, he was on his knees when he got to the net and he beat me with a shot to the high corner."

The goalie who faced Richard the most was his teammate Jacques Plante, who was the team's practice goalie while playing senior hockey in Montreal before he became an NHL all-star.

"In practice he was as serious about scoring as in games, and I was just as serious about stopping him," Plante said. *"If I stopped him a couple of times in a row, he often would break his stick over the boards.*

"He was a big help to my goaltending because early in my time as a practice goalie, he pointed out some things I was doing that left openings for him to shoot at. As I gained experience and stopped him a few times on breakaways, it really made him sore because he regarded all goalies as the enemy. Finally, he paid me the large compliment of asking what he was doing that tipped me off to what his move might be. I told him that when he carried the puck ahead of him on a break, it meant he intended to stickhandle it into the net. If he carried it to his left, he planned to shoot.

"After that, he took great delight in coming at me with the puck to his left, then doing that spin of his to deliver a backhand."

Johnny Bower, who gave up Rocket's final career goal, and Glenn Hall, who allowed Richard's number 500, were admirers when they spoke with Dick Irvin Jr., as he reported in his book, *In the Crease, Goaltenders look at life in the NHL.*

"I tried to size him up, but I couldn't", Bower complained.

"He'd score on me through my legs, then another along the ice, then on one side, and then the other side. He had me going crazy. The biggest thrill of my life was when he retired."

Hall concurred. *"What a competitor he was. The Rocket forced you to play the whole 60 minutes. You knew that with 58 minutes gone in the game, you had to play him full out in the last two. He wouldn't quit."*

Bill Durnan and the Rocket

"As unimportant as junior hockey was in the scheme of things, the senior Royals in the Quebec league were almost as popular as the NHL Canadiens. Many times the Royals' Sunday afternoon games would outdraw what the Canadiens had the night before.

"They played in a league that was very wide open. There was almost no back-checking and there were several ex-NHL players who were very stylish and who could put on a good show for the fans... The senior Royals won the Allan Cup in 1947. Oddly enough, the fellows who came out of that team and who were supposed to make the Canadiens were not capable of doing it. With the exception of Doug Harvey and Floyd Curry and Gerry McNeil who came along a year or two later and was a classy goal-tender, none of them was able to stick in the NHL."

Selke had to start below senior hockey, at the midget, juvenile and junior levels. Selke immediately set up a feeder system of junior and senior league teams in Quebec, as well as spending money on amateur hockey in Regina, Winnipeg and Edmonton, among other centres, to ensure that Maurice Richard would be surrounded with talent when his veteran teammates retired.

Even superstar goal scorers have to play defence every now and then.

A Model for Success

Maurice Richard was Selke's model, but not only for his skills on the ice. Frank Selke's beliefs in family values were deeply entrenched. He was impressed by the Rocket and his relationships with his family and the community.

Soon players from the Quebec Citadelles, the Nationals, Junior Canadiens, Verdun-LaSalle Cyclones, Montreal Royals and other junior teams in a much-improved Quebec league, were working their way toward the Forum.

"I purposely operated the farm clubs like a farmer," he said. *"I always liked to spot good potential players, like plants, coming up and helped them to develop and ripen in the system until they were good enough to come up.*

"We were the first to do it. We helped teams everywhere. In Winnipeg we had 10 teams, in Regina we financed the whole amateur system, and in Edmonton, we spent up to $300,000 a year in amateur development. And we were able to do it because we sold $200,000 worth of good players every season out of it."

The managing director's strategy began working as soon as it was implemented. Rocket's impact on the ice attracted new French-speaking talent to the club almost immediately.

APRIL 14, 1956

The team that dines together, wins together. Claude Provost, Maurice, Henri Richard and Jean Béliveau celebrate the 1956 Stanley Cup. The practice of wearing team jackets ended in the 1960s.

I purposely operated the farm clubs like a farmer.

– Frank Selke

Suzanne Richard, 2, tweaks daddy's nose under the watchful eye of mom Lucille and big sister Huguette.

Maurice Richard always had a designated checker "in his pocket".

Opposing Forwards and Defencemen

The statements from NHL stars about trying to stop Maurice Richard say it all about his ability, strength and passion for scoring.

"The fiercest, most electrifying competitor I ever faced seldom said a word on the ice because the Rocket spoke with his eyes," said Bill Gadsby, a star NHL defenceman for 20 years.

Ted Lindsay, the brilliant left-winger of the Detroit Red Wings, was Richard's most bitter rival, their battles a major chapter in hockey's folklore. Neither man spoke a good word about the other during their playing days, but after they both were long out of the game, a few compliments surfaced.

"Rocket was the master of pacing himself," Lindsay said. *"One minute, he would seem to be skating aimlessly, then he would get an opening, strike and you were dead. Beautiful!"*

Red Kelly was on four Stanley Cup champion teams as a defenceman with the Detroit Red Wings, and four more at centre with the Toronto Maple Leafs.

"I played on the Rocket's side of the ice, and when he came down against me, he was dynamite, the hardest guy to stop in my career," Kelly said. *"He was a left-hand shot playing right wing and he would come like a jet down the wing and make that incredible right angle cut to the net. When you tried to stop him, he had such strength that he could grab your stick with one hand and shove you aside. Trying to stop him getting to the net was the toughest task I ever faced in hockey because he was so quick and strong."*

Gadsby claimed that the Rocket seldom cut to the middle against him.

"He would try to move me to the outside towards the boards and then cut in behind me." Gadsby said. *"That's the move I wanted most players to make, one that I seemed to handle well. But the Rocket wasn't 'most players'. He had that great balance and strength. He could ward me off with one arm and bring up the puck with one hand on the stick."*

Hal Laycoe, first as a teammate, and later as a controversial opponent of the Rocket, had a unique take on Richard.

"Nobody ever played the game with as much emotion as he had," he said. *"I think he was the most emotional hockey player who ever lived, and he used it as a strength."*

Lindsay claims that he and Richard shared an intense desire to win and that meant one of the bitterest conflicts ever in any sport.

"We detested – yes, hated – each other from the start and I would do anything I could to upset him, taunting him, calling him names about his ancestry, anything to get him off his game and help us win," Lindsay said. *"He gave it to me good a few times.*

"From the blue line in, he was the best player who ever lived. He could skate, he was strong, he was mean and he focused on the net like no other."

"I was living, breathing and eating hockey 24 hours a day," wrote Bernard Geoffrion with Stan Fischler in *Boom Boom*. *"When the Canadiens' games were on the radio I would listen for every mention of the Rocket. For me, nobody could be bigger than Maurice Richard and when he scored, the roar of the crowd was music to my ears."*

Geoffrion, who would patent the slapshot, hence his nickname, was able to tell his idol about his dreams to follow him to the Forum while still a youth.

"Rocket used to train by riding his bicycle and his route often took him past my father's restaurant in Bordeaux, a Montreal district," Geoffrion said. *"He began dropping by the restaurant and I was there one day when the Rocket happened to stop in. My father introduced me and I said to him: 'Mr. Richard, you are my idol. I listen to you on the radio all the time. I am going to work hard and I want to be just like you.' He responded by saying: 'I hope you make it one day, kid.' "*

"Hat Trick" celebration in the Canadiens dressing room.
⌄

When Maurice Richard scored, the roar
of the crowd was music to my ears.

– Bernard Geoffrion

Farmer Frank's Reconstruction

53

Farther away in the Quebec heartland of Victoriaville, a teen-aged Jean Béliveau also was swept away by French Canada's greatest hero.

"I was just one of thousands of young hockey players who sat rapt by the family radio on Saturday nights, letting my imagination magnify the Rocket's epic feats on La Soirée du Hockey, *then mimicking those same actions on the local rink on crisp Sunday mornings after Mass,"* Gros Bill said.

"Later as his teammate, this sense of awe remained. As an adult, the realization that Maurice opened it up for us — built it for us — was almost overwhelming. Even more impressive was the fact that he was rather shy, and very modest about his exploits."

Frank Selke was right in his approach to made-in-Quebec players. The generation of homegrown stars who shared a dressing room with the Rocket in the 1950s would crash through walls to win, just as Richard would, because they, like he, knew what it meant to wear the *Sainte-Flanelle*, the Holy Cloth that bore the CH on its crest.

Just as important to the team's success was a complete renovation of the Forum in 1949, which increased seating capacity to more than 13,000 and helped provide some of the revenues that paid for the farm system Selke had put together.

A compound leg fracture ends Toe Blake's playing career... and the Punch Line.

While Selke built up that system, the NHL Canadiens relied on a veteran team of such stars as Kenny Reardon and Butch Bouchard on defence, Bill Durnan in goal and Toe Blake, Elmer Lach, Buddy O'Connor, Billy Reay and Kenny Mosdell up front.

When Blake went down with a compound fracture of his ankle in a 3-1 loss to the Rangers at Madison Square Garden on Jan. 11, 1948, the Canadiens' fortunes went with him, and the team finished fifth, missing the playoffs by four points. A year later, after Lach, Bouchard and Reardon missed substantial segments of the schedule with injuries, the Canadiens managed to place third before losing their semi-final in seven games to Detroit.

Doug Harvey had joined the team, and westerners Tom Johnson and Bob Turner would help solidify the blue line throughout the 1950s. One judicious trade, speedster Leo Gravelle and cash to Chicago for strapping left-winger Bert Olmstead, ended the talent search for Toe Blake's replacement, three years after his retirement.

THE STALWART

Butch Bouchard was the glue that held the Canadiens together in the 1940s and early '50s. He and Maurice Richard shared four Stanley Cups together.

Farmer Frank's Reconstruction

But it wouldn't be until Frank Selke's pipeline was pumping at full capacity that the Canadiens would turn the 1950s into the National Hockey League's one-team show.

Within five years, he would completely restock his team and would surround Maurice Richard with the kind of Quebec-raised talent that would skate to multiple Stanley Cups: Béliveau, Henri Richard, Geoffrion, Dickie Moore, Jean-Claude Tremblay, Gilles Tremblay, Jean-Guy Talbot, Donnie Marshall, Claude Provost, Phil Goyette and Jacques Plante.

With the Rocket and Moore flanking Henri Richard on one line, and Béliveau pivoting Geoffrion and Olmstead, the Canadiens would possess the most powerful offence the league had ever seen. And with Harvey, Johnson, Talbot and Turner anchoring the blue line in front of Plante, the team featured one of the stingiest defences in the NHL.

The 1946-47 Canadiens
v

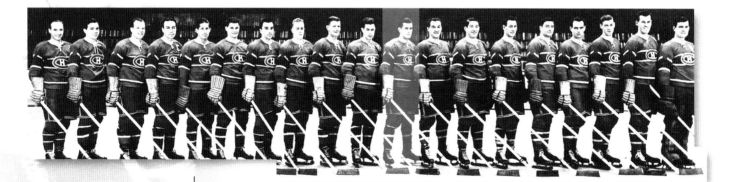

The Teammates

∧
Maurice and the "Old Guard" celebrate a win in the late 1940s.

While controversy and a wide range of viewpoints on the athlete and the man were a big part of Maurice Richard's hockey career, those who were his teammates with the Montreal Canadiens were unanimous: The Rocket was an extraordinary athlete, a peerless leader, a strong and loyal friend.

"He was a good man, very reserved and quiet," said Ray Getliffe, a Canadiens winger for the first three seasons of Richard's career. *"There were no problems, no negatives in his life and when he got on the ice, he was raw power, speed and emotion."*

Already a star when he joined the Canadiens from the Quebec Aces in 1953 after a three-year "holdout" to stay in senior amateur hockey, Jean Béliveau quickly discovered a fact of Canadiens' life.

"When I first arrived in Montreal, the Canadiens may have been managed by Frank Selke, but they were Maurice Richard's team," Béliveau said. *"The Rocket was the heart and soul of the Canadiens and an inspiration to us all, especially to younger French-Canadians who were rising through the ranks. He was man and myth, larger than life in some ways, yet most ordinarily human in others.*

"The timing of his contributions, from the war years through to 1960, coincided with the period in Quebec when a tidal wave of change was sweeping aside more than 300 years of history. Maurice Richard represented success against great odds. French-Canadians who had little interest in hockey understood this clearly and his example was brought before his countrymen in many forums."

Elmer Lach, from Saskatchewan, the centre on the mighty Punch Line with Richard and Toe Blake, was Richard's roommate on the road for many seasons.

"Maurice was fun to go golfing with in the summer and a great fisherman who knew the best spots to catch'em in northern Quebec," Lach said. *"But he never relaxed for a second in the hockey season."*

Lach laughed when he revealed a "secret" of Richard's success. *"The Rocket would sleep 12 hours a day,"* Lach said. *"Maybe that's why he had so much energy on the ice."*

Goalie **Jacques Plante** made a serious study of Richard and was a big booster.

"Maybe I'm prejudiced because I played 400 NHL games watching him from a good viewing point," Plante said. *"Maybe Gordie Howe was better, maybe Bobby Hull, maybe Phil Esposito or Jean Béliveau. But I know one thing without a doubt: If I needed one big goal and could pick any player in history, I would grab the Rocket."*

In Plante's view, Richard led by example. *"The Rocket was a very quiet man and on the road trips, he would watch us play cards and laugh at the jokes,"* Plante said. *"He always took the blame himself for a loss, never faulting anyone else. If a player wasn't working hard enough or playing smart, one glare from the Rocket usually corrected the problem."*

BATTLE OF THE 9s

Comparison of great athletes is among

sport's biggest appeals, in the endless discus-

sions and arguments as to which performer

brings the most to the competitive table. Hockey

has had several long-running confrontations

between individuals who were the main contenders

for various honors and all-star spots through many

seasons in their careers. But none inspired as much

controversy for as long as Maurice Richard and Gordie

Howe. Perhaps the only comparable situation was the Ted

Williams vs. Joe DiMaggio baseball debate that raged on

through their long careers. **9**

Their very different styles helped to fuel the Richard-Howe argument. The mercurial Richard, always high-strung and appearing ready to explode with a goal or violence in a heartbeat, was the NHL's most electrifying performer. Howe played with such efficiency and ease that he often appeared not to be trying very hard when, in reality, he was.

Red Burnett, who covered the NHL for the *Toronto Star* through much of the time when the two great wingers were in the league, offered a wise assessment of them.

"You had to watch Howe closely and count all the little parts of the game that he did so well, a steal of the puck here, a smart little pass there, a strong check in his own zone or a long retention of the puck when he was killing a penalty," Burnett said. *"At the end of the night, you would have a long list of positives.*

"Through much of the same game, you would not have noticed the Rocket, although you always had your eye out for him because you didn't want to miss the explosion. Then in a sudden move, one of those sweeps around a defenceman, holding the opponent off with one hand and bringing the puck with the other hand on the stick, then cutting to the net for a goal, Rocket would be what you remembered about the game."

Burnett had a favorite story about the Rocket's fabled attitude that only what the team did mattered, not individual performance.

"The Canadiens and the Leafs had tied, 4-4, in a 1947 game at Maple Leaf Gardens, and all the Rocket did was score three great goals and assist on the fourth," Burnett recalled. *"We were using more pictures on the sports pages and wanted one of him for the next day's paper so I took a photographer into the dressing room after the game. I asked Richard if he would kiss the stick he used, he glared at me and said: 'Kiss the blankety-blank thing yourself! We didn't win, did we?'"*

The Leafs were very attentive when the Rocket was around.

The Rocket would be what you remember about the game.

– Red Burnett, Toronto Star

Their NHL careers overlapped for 14 seasons, from Howe's debut as an 18-year-old in 1945, to Richard's retirement in 1960. In that stretch, the two players each earned 11 all-star team nominations, six first-team selections for the Rocket, seven for Howe. In one nine-season stretch, they were one-two in right-wing voting eight times, including six consecutive seasons from 1948-49 to 1953-54.

The Richard-Howe argument did not hinge on who was the best all-round player — most conceded that honor to Howe — but on value to their teams. While Richard might not be the thorough, do-it-all winger for 200 feet of ice, his ability to score goals under pressure (82 playoff scores, 18 of them winners, six overtime scores) and the teeth-clenched leadership he supplied, raised him to the very top level, albeit by a slightly different path than the one Howe travelled to that point.

The familiar faces of Howe and Richard graced 22 NHL all-star teams.

Chasing the First Big Record

^
At this point in the season, Maurice had scored 30 (count'em) goals, enough to form his first initial.

There was a rare air of excitement as the new National Hockey League season got under way in late October 1952.

The league's career scoring record of 324 goals held by former Maroons captain Nels *Old Poison* Stewart was only five goals away for Maurice Richard, and the countdown in the local media began with the opening face-off to the new season.

The Rocket promptly went six games without a goal.

The pressure eased off when the Canadiens tied the Blackhawks at two on October 23 and the Rocket scored both goals. Two nights later, Montreal overwhelmed Terry Sawchuk and the Red Wings, 9-0, and the Rocket scored again.

The Canadiens travelled to Toronto for a Maple Leaf Gardens tilt on October 29 and the local dailies jumped into the fray, with *The Telegram*, *Globe* and *Mail* and *Daily Star* all featuring the countdown on page one. When the team arrived at their hotel, journalists and fans instantly mobbed them, and a phalanx of players quickly surrounded Richard and whisked him away to his room, far from the madding crowd.

None of the speculating journalists wasted their prognostications on a single tally to approach the record. No, the outstanding question of the day was whether the Rocket would score twice to tie the record, or three times to set his own. Needless to say, the 14,069 blue-and-white faithful greeted his offensive efforts with cascades of boos, only cheering when rookie defenceman Tim Horton sent him sprawling with a trip early in the first period.

The animus of the Toronto crowd was exactly the tonic Richard needed. Eleven minutes into the game, Richard accepted a pass from Elmer Lach, quickly skirted the defence and deftly defeated goalie Harry Lumley for goal number 323.

Six minutes later, he took two defencemen and a forward into Lumley's crease and the puck trickled into the net. The Toronto fans, to their credit, gave the Rocket a loud ovation, but were disappointed when he was shut out the rest of the way in a 7-5 loss.

Maurice Richard went three games without a goal, and the Forum faithful were on the edges of their seats on November 8, when the Blackhawks visited. Early in the second period, linemate Elmer Lach was credited with his 200th career goal, and the first of a pair he would score that night. A few moments later, the Rocket shot the puck toward Al Rollins in the Chicago net, just as a defenceman took down winger Bert Olmstead in the crease. The puck appeared to touch Olmstead, but Red Storey immediately pointed toward Richard and the Forum went wild. It was the 10th anniversary of Richard's first NHL goal.

After the game, the team streamed into the dressing room and hardly noticed that all of the wastebaskets had been dented and strewn about. Olmstead had got there first, and taken out his frustrations on the room. Not only had he scored Richard's record marker, he had shot Lach's 200th in off a Chicago defender, only to have Storey award the goal to Lach.

After the Richard goal, the teams lined up for the face-off, and a Chicago winger asked Olmstead: *"Why didn't you tell them it was your goal?"* The whole Chicago bench knew who had scored.

"I'd get shot if I did," Olmstead replied. So instead of a hat trick, Big Bert from Sceptre, Saskatchewan, had to be content with one goal, on a night when nobody would remember it.

As for the Rocket, now that he had scored number 325, he would never chase another record. From now on, he'd set all the career marks that others would seek to overtake.

Red Storey, himself an excellent all-round athlete especially in football and lacrosse, was a referee during Richard's and Howe's glitter days in the 1950s. His assessment of the two stars is perhaps the one adopted most often by those who looked closely at them.

"Hockey fans argued more about who was the best, Gordie or the Rocket, than any other two players in history," Storey said. *"I was asked often and I told anyone who asked that Rocket Richard was the greatest goal scorer and the most exciting player the world has ever seen. Then I would say that Gordie Howe was the greatest player in history. I would say that they were two different people and nobody had the talent of Howe and nobody has the scoring ability of the Rocket. I'm not sure if I pleased everybody, or nobody, but that's the way I felt."*

Red Kelly had perhaps the best chance of any NHLer to assess the two players. Kelly spent 21 seasons in the NHL, 13 of them with the Red Wings as a defenceman, playing with Howe and against the Rocket in their many historical playoff series. He was traded to the Toronto Maple Leafs in February 1960, and switched to centre where he excelled for eight seasons.

In Roy MacSkimming's excellent unauthorized biography, *Gordie: A Hockey Legend*, Kelly discussed the two great wingers: *"Gordie was powerful, and he could do lots of things on the ice,"* Kelly said. *"He could be mean – the elbows and the whole deal. I saw him break a guy's nose once when we played the Rangers. Not a very big guy but he'd been whacking Gordie on the shins and Gordie told him to leave him alone. Suddenly the guy comes on the ice and whump, he's down with a broken nose. No penalty or anything, nobody knows what happened, the referees never saw it. But that was Gordie.*

WAR ON THE LINKS

Habs vs. Leafs on the links: Elmer Lach and Maurice take on Toronto's Jim Thomson and Teeder Kennedy.

"Gordie was different from the Rocket. On a given occasion, the Rocket could rise to greater heights. All-round, Gordie would be the best. But the Rocket could be more dynamic."

During his time as coach of the Maple Leafs, Kelly was asked about the rivalry between the Red Wings and the Canadiens in the 1950s. The Wings won the Stanley Cup in 1952, '54 and '55, the latter two in seven-game series. The Canadiens replied in 1953, and then the record five consecutive crowns from '56 to '60.

"The teams were so evenly matched until later in the '50s that a lucky bounce could decide the Cup," Kelly said. *"In the seventh game in 1954, Gaye Stewart (Canadiens) hit our post with a minute to go, then Tony Leswick won it for us in overtime. In 1955, when we were tied well into the third period of the seventh game, the Canadiens did not score on four very good chances and we were able to win. With a couple of breaks, they could have won eight Stanley Cups in a row."*

Red Storey had several run-ins with the Rocket during their careers. He never quit trying to reform the feisty winger, however.
ˇ

All-round, Gordie would be the best.

But the Rocket would be the most dynamic.

– Red Kelly

The only way to end the season:
Elmer Lach, Butch Bouchard and the
Rocket share the 1953 Cup victory.

Frank Selke had to walk a careful line in assessing the two great wingers because the Rocket had led Selke's team to great success. But after Richard retired, Selke did discuss the matter in an interview with Vern DeGeer of *The Gazette*.

"*Gordie Howe is the finest all-round player in the history of hockey,*" Selke told DeGeer.

"*I'm not taking anything away from the Rocket, or any other player when I say this. A couple of years ago, King Clancy (in the NHL as a player, referee and executive for 70 years) put it this way: 'If there were two rinks in Montreal offering games at the same time with Howe and Richard as box office rivals, the Rocket would do more business.' Richard was the game's greatest crowd pleaser, the most spectacular goal-getter, but Howe can do more things than any player that ever lived. And I know the Rocket thinks the same way.*"

THE HALLOWED SILVERWARE

When Maurice Richard retired in 1960, he had eight Stanley Cup wins under his belt, a league record. Other Canadiens, including brother Henri (11) and Jean Béliveau (10) would later surpass that mark.

A Mutual Admiration Society

How did the two great players view each other? Through their years as NHL peers, Richard and Howe were bitter rivals on teams that simply did not like each other, playing some of the most intense, violent games in history. While they were both in action, Howe said little while Richard would both praise and criticize Howe in the same sentence.

"Howe is a great player, the best I ever played against, but he should hustle more," said Richard near the end of his career. *"He doesn't seem to be trying as hard as he could. He was a better all-round player than I was, maybe the best ever. But I think he should have scored more big goals, like in the playoffs."*

The biggest source of pride in Richard's career was his playoff excellence, the time when his goals really mattered because they brought honors to the team. He scored 82 goals in 133 playoff games, including six overtime winners. Howe had 68 goals in 157 playoff matches, and it's a surprise to many to learn that he did not count an OT score, although the Wings went to extra time in 22 playoff games during Howe's time in Detroit.

Two More Milestones: Goals 400 and 500

Al Rollins, who spent eight seasons in the NHL with Chicago, Toronto and New York and was one of only four goaltenders to win the Hart Trophy as most valuable player, once joked that his real job was "to be the victim of Maurice Richard's milestone goals."

Rollins was the Blackhawks goalie in November 1952, when Richard scored career goal No. 325 to surpass the mark set by Nels *Old Poison* Stewart, a standard that had endured for 22 years.

Then, on December 18, 1954, Rollins was in goal for the Hawks in a game at Chicago when the Rocket counted the 400th goal of his career, setting off a loud celebration by the Canadiens players amid mild applause from the Chicago Stadium fans.

"At least this time, there wasn't a 10-minute ovation as there was the night in Montreal when Richard set the career record," Rollins said.

Richard had started the 1954-55 season with 384 goals and needed 32 games to produce the 16 scores he needed for the 400 mark. He opened the schedule slowly, scoreless in the first six games.

The Rocket played in 176 games before he reached the next plateau, 500 goals, in the 1957-58 season. Starting the season seven goals short of the milestone, he wasted no time in getting the job done, scaling that lofty height in six games, wrapping it up in a week.

Richard found the magic figure on October 19 at the Forum when he took a pass from Jean Béliveau and beat Blackhawks goalie Glenn Hall to set off another long ovation by his fans.

After the game the Rocket dedicated the puck from No. 500 to Dick Irvin Sr., his long-time coach who had died earlier that year.

"He was the man who taught me everything I know about hockey," Richard said that night.

Less than a month later, Richard found the other emotional extreme. He suffered a cut Achilles tendon just above the heel and was out of action for 42 games.

^
On December 19, 1954, the Rocket receives a Plouffe family reception from actors Émile Genest and Pierre Valcour, two series' regulars, after scoring number 400.

(Top left)
When the team train pulled in to Windsor Station, hundreds of fans were waiting for the Rocket.

The Goal

If ever there was a frustrating season for Maurice Richard it was the 1951-52 campaign.

Bernard Geoffrion scored twice and the Rocket added another in a 4-2 win over Chicago on opening night and optimism reigned in Montreal. However, Detroit proved to be the team of the regular season, and began to pull away from the Leafs and Canadiens at mid-season.

On December 31, the Canadiens scored their first win against the Red Wings in eight starts, 5-3, with the Rocket netting his nineteenth goal of the year, and Gordie Howe turning in a hat trick in a losing cause.

The Rocket went scoreless over the next four games, and then scored a hat trick of his own in an 8-3 win over Chicago. On February 6, a limping Richard was taken out of the line-up and sent to Florida for rest and rehabilitation. He finished the season with 27 goals, fourth best in the league, a feat considering 22 games missed, but he was on shaky pins as the playoffs got under way.

The Canadiens struggled against the third-place Bruins in the semi-final, and would have been eliminated in six games had it not been for an overtime goal by Paul Masnick at the Garden.

Early in the second period of game seven, the Rocket tried his patented "button-hook" around Boston defender Hal Laycoe. Bruins forward Leo Labine cut behind Laycoe from the other side and hit Richard low and sent him crashing head-first to the ice. The Forum was deathly silent as a groggy, bleeding Richard was conveyed to the clinic.

Only five minutes remained when Richard skated slowly to his team's bench, his head down, a towel around his neck.

"Can you go?" coach Irvin asked, practically convinced that Richard was concussed. Richard had adamantly refused a ride to the hospital for x-rays suggested by the team doctor; he nodded, and said, curtly: *"Sure."*

"Okay, get out there."

Four minutes remained in regulation time when Richard took the puck from Butch Bouchard deep in his zone and evaded Fleming Mackell at the blue line. He eluded Woody Dumart and another Bruins forward in the neutral zone, and broke into the Boston end. He tried to angle big defenceman Bill Quackenbush into the middle, driving him into his partner, Bob Armstrong, but Quackenbush was stronger and forced the Rocket wide and towards the corner.

Suddenly, the Rocket leaned back on the defender, pushing him off with his arm and cutting to the Boston goal. Armstrong cut over and Richard button-hooked him, and moved in on Sugar Jim Henry, who as Andy O'Brien recollected *"was squinting through a mess of a face that had suffered a broken nose and two black eyes earlier in the series."*

Richard faked Henry to the ice and put the puck into the net with what some observers called the "Goal of the Century." The Canadiens won 2-1 and the picture of the two wounded gladiators, Richard and Henry, in the post-series handshake is a sports classic *(above left)*.

What the fans didn't know was that once Richard returned to the dressing room at game's end, he broke into wild, sobbing convulsions. Teammates rushed to his side, holding down his thrashing arms and legs, and team doctor Gordon Young administered a powerful sedative. Fully two hours passed before the Rocket was sufficiently recovered to go home.

When Howe was in his final campaign, a return to the NHL from the World Hockey Association with the Hartford Whalers in the 1979-80 season, Richard was asked about Gordie's playing at 52 years of age.

"Players learn to play when they're young and that's how they play all their lives," Richard said. *"There are a lot of skills this generation doesn't have. They know they don't have to stickhandle, just chase after the puck. It may be that today's game is faster; it may be there's more skating, but teams just throw the puck in and chase it. The game's become a foot race. I guess that's another reason Gordie's still going."*

In 1964, four years after Richard retired, the *Miami Herald* carried a series in which 10 champion athletes chose the best ever in their sports. Richard was the hockey selector, and he picked Howe, delivering a glowing tribute to his long-time rival.

"He (Howe) is the best player now and has been for 16 years," the Rocket wrote. *"Part of the beauty of Howe's play is that he does so many positive things without seeming to make hardly an effort. Yet to do the things he does he must make a tremendous effort. He is the complete hockey player."*

Maurice gives goal-scoring lessons to several teammates and a Boston goalie, Red Henry.
ˇ

Howe's reply indicated that the two long-time combatants had formed a mutual admiration society.

"The NHL never had a more dramatic player than the Rocket, nor one more dangerous in the clutch," Howe said.

The "mystery" Richard cultivated about himself was mentioned by his old linemate Toe Blake.

"I considered the Rocket to be an old friend but I really wasn't that close to him, not the open way most friends are," Blake once said. *"He never revealed much of himself. I think he felt that if people knew a lot about him personally, they would know his weaknesses and take advantage of them."*

At Richard's funeral, Howe expressed surprise when he learned facts about Richard.

"Is it true he had seven children?" Howe asked. *"I never knew that. You never really knew what the man was thinking. He was a quiet man. On the ice, I would say 'Hi Rocket', and he would just growl at me. I didn't know him too well but I don't think his brother Henri knew him too well either."*

Howe was asked if he thought the Rocket enjoyed the game.

"If he did," Howe replied, *"he didn't show it."*

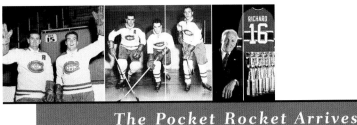

The Pocket Rocket Arrives

^
When Henri Richard ended his 20-year career, he had been part of teams that won 11 Stanley Cups, an individual record that should never be challenged.

With the Rocket in full flight, and with Quebec junior league products Dickie Moore, Bernard Geoffrion, Jacques Plante and Jean Béliveau forging stellar National Hockey League careers, most of the hockey focus in Quebec was on the NHL Canadiens.

Henri Richard, 15 years younger than big brother Maurice, was built smaller at five-feet, seven-inches and 160 wiry pounds, but when the 19-year-old arrived at the NHL team's camp in September 1955, his tryout was considered a courtesy to the Rocket.

It soon became evident that Richard the Younger did not see this as a quick skate with the big boys before he returned, "where he belonged" – junior hockey. Veteran observers quickly realized that the rookie was taking this opportunity to make the team seriously.

"Nobody can get the puck away from Henri Richard," former defenceman Ken Reardon reported to Frank Selke.

"Yes, but he's very small," Selke replied. The diminutive managing director liked his players large.

Jean Béliveau was a very big centre, 11 inches taller and 50 pounds heavier than the Pocket Rocket. Three years into his NHL career, he was already the best at his position in the league.

"He may be small, Mr. Selke, but I'm having a heckuva time trying to play against him, and so is everybody else. He needs to stay here, I think," Béliveau suggested.

"Sending him back to junior is dangerous," said big brother Maurice. *"They know he's my brother and they gang up on him. He's safer in the NHL. Although you don't have to worry about Henri, Mr. Selke, he's as tough as they come."*

The Rocket got to prove that point rather painfully before camp was out. Selke was busy with paperwork when a team trainer burst into his office: *"Mr. Selke, come quick! Richard has been knocked out!"*

"Which one?"

"Both of them!" the trainer exclaimed. In a team scrimmage, Rocket zigged and Henri zagged. Splat.

Rocket came to on the trainer's table, with a concerned Henri hovering over him holding an ice bag to a newly stitched (five) cut on his forehead. Pocket Rocket, being shorter, had cut under big brother and caught him a beaut when their heads clashed.

"I think Maurice had about 15 stitches from that one," Henri recalled much later.

Maurice shook out the cobwebs and sat up, looking sternly at his younger brother.

"Henri, you gotta watch out; you could get hurt out there," he advised, all fraternal concern.

A couple weeks later, big brother Maurice accompanied the unilingual Henri to his first contract negotiation with the unilingual Frank Selke Sr.

"How much does he want?" Selke asked.

"The money doesn't matter Mr. Selke," Big Brother dutifully translated. *"He just wants to play with the Canadiens."* The brothers put their heads together and conferred some more.

"How about a $2,000 signing bonus and the rookie rate, $100 a game ($7,000 a year)?" Maurice suggested.

Selke pulled out a contract, filled in the figures, and both parties signed. The Richard brothers were heading for the door when Selke called them back.

"He took back the contract, tore it up and increased my signing bonus to $5,000. He told Maurice that he didn't want me later on thinking that he had taken advantage of my youth. He didn't know that I was ready to pay him for playing with the Canadiens," Henri recalled.

Selke confirmed the story: *"I felt certain that the boy was going to make it and in years to come, I didn't want him to feel I had taken advantage of his youth and eagerness. He has received much better contracts since, and there never have been any arguments."*

"I could sign a Richard a day," he smiled, *"if they delivered players like Maurice and Henri."*

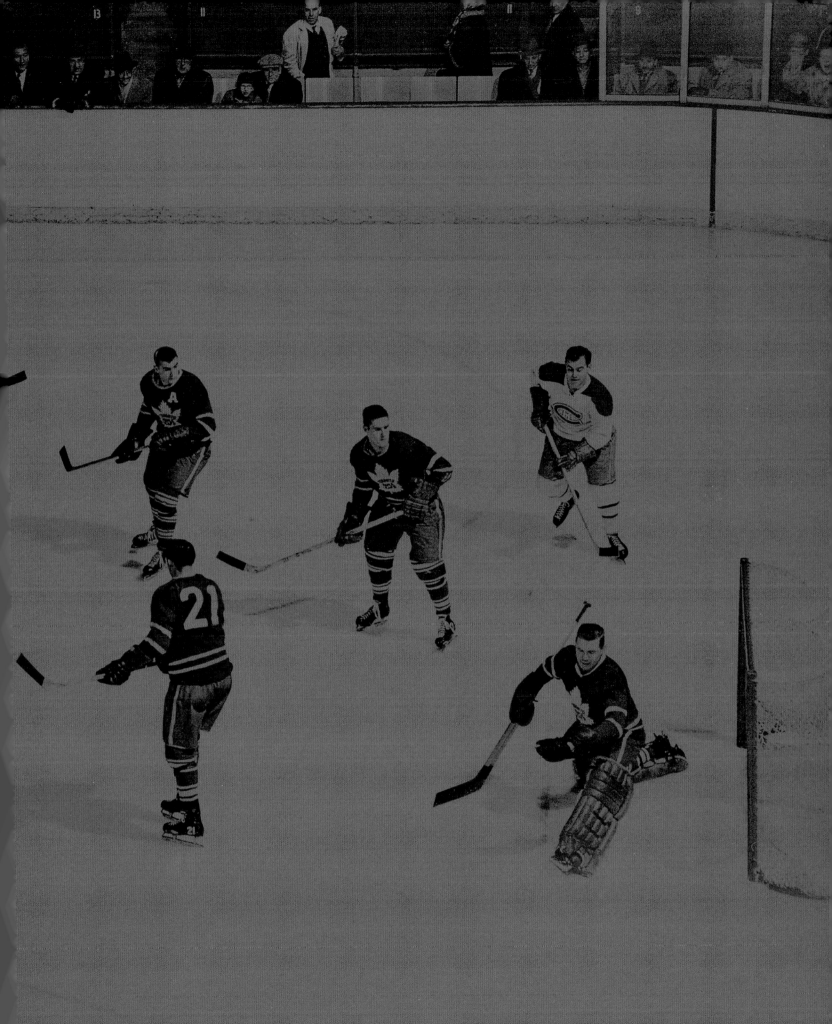

The Rocket beats the world: all six Toronto players are beaten on this goal by Maurice Richard.

THE RIOT

*I*n retrospect, nothing was more predictable than the explosion by Maurice Richard, in a game in Boston, in March, 1955. Except, perhaps, National Hockey League president Clarence Campbell throwing the book at him, at the behest of the other teams in the league. The repercussions of a simple hockey fight would go far beyond the NHL, and would still be felt almost a half-century later. **9**

J ust as predictable, if not even more so, was the reaction by French Canadians as they took to the streets in collective anger on St. Patrick's Day and trashed downtown Montreal. It had been building for years. Diverse observers such as American sportswriter Herbert Warren Wind, writing in the new *Sports Illustrated*, and Canadian writer Hugh MacLennan, author of *Two Solitudes*, had both alluded to it in articles published a few months before.

And three months before the events of that spring, there was an incident in Toronto. Red Storey was officiating a holiday week tilt between the Canadiens and Leafs, which was tied, 1-1, in the final minutes. Rookie defenceman Bob Bailey cracked the Rocket into the boards with a heavy, but legal check. As Storey reported, *"The Rocket had been taking abuse all night, which was nothing new. You were going to be abused if you were that good a goal scorer, and he would take as much as he could. Then, without warning, he would explode."*

When players weren't grabbing and clutching the Rocket, he was making life miserable for goalies.
⌄

Richard chased after Bailey and slammed into the Leaf rearguard, stick up. Bailey lost the crowns of two teeth in the collision, and the pair fell to the ice in a vicious, clawing tangle. Storey and linesman George Hayes, a gentle giant of six-feet, three-inches, 230 pounds, kept separating the pair and disarming the Rocket, but Richard kept coming back swinging at Bailey with a new stick.

"We didn't find out until we looked at the film later that the Canadiens' coach, the late Dick Irvin Sr., was giving Richard a new stick every time we got him disarmed and over to the bench. That happened five times. The Rocket also slapped George once while he was trying to break it up, and he got his glove into my face a couple of times. The Rocket had a temper but he really wasn't a bad guy and hadn't done much damage, so George and I tried to soften it up in our report."

Toronto president Conn Smythe sent film of the incident to league president Clarence Campbell, but without special mention by the game officials in the game report, Campbell could only fine Richard $250 and elicit a promise of better behavior in the future. Later that season, Detroit's Ted Lindsay got involved in a similar situation and was suspended for 10 games.

The scene was set for an incident that would stand the hockey world on its collective ear.

APRIL 1955

Maurice Richard, Elmer Lach and Toe Blake attend a special "Old Timers" fundraiser in Ottawa for Tommy Gorman.

The Rocket had a temper but he wasn't a bad guy and hadn't done much damage, so I tried to soften it up in our report.

– Red Storey

MACLEAN'S MAGAZINE

A Hero for Quebec

By Hugh MacLennan

January 15, 1955

Hugh MacLennan was the first major English writer to tackle Canada's national character in his work. In Two Solitudes (1945), he wrote about English-French tensions in Quebec during the First World War, and his seminal work was much quoted by other writers in the period of The Quiet Revolution.

A professor at McGill for more than thirty years, MacLennan won the Governor General's Literary Award more than any other Canadian author, three times for fiction and twice for nonfiction.

He died in Montreal in 1990, at age 83.

I don't think I'm fanciful in my belief that 1954 was a year of change in Montreal.

At the moment, Canada has no real focal point, partly because we are a bilingual nation but also because the issue between Montreal and Toronto remains undecided. At stake in this inter-city rivalry is the privilege of setting the style for our growing country, and Montrealers are beginning to fear that the geographical and economic cards are stacked against them, just as they fear the mentality of Toronto is better adjusted to the modern age than their own.

Montreal's current enthusiasm for a hockey player called Maurice Richard is probably not unconnected with the city's awareness that its prestige is being challenged. Richard has become the greatest hero Montreal has ever acknowledged and it is obvious that his genius for hockey is only a partial cause of his apotheosis.

In many ways, Howie Morenz was a greater forward, and today Béliveau and Geoffrion are probably more useful to the team. But, as one sportswriter put it, the Rocket is terrific even while standing still.

He is more interesting when he misses a goal than most men when they connect. And when he does put the puck into the net, the Forum thunders with approval of something more than a change in the score.

It is admiration for the man himself, an identification of the city's spirit with his. For Richard is an old-fashioned personality, utterly non-conformist, relying more on élan than on cunning, with a strange courtliness even in his ferocity. There is no trace in him of the good mixer or great guy, no pretence of being just like everyone else, no false modesty, no deliberate showmanship, no cheap appeals for popularity. He is a passionate individual.

It is to this old-fashioned individualism that Montreal responds. When Richard returned from Chicago after scoring his four hundredth goal, he was met by a mob of enthusiasts stretching out their hands to touch him. In his honour they carried a towering *papier-mâché* effigy of their hero that looked like one of those grotesque mediaeval images seen in Mardi Gras parades in the south of France. An anachronism in the middle of the 20th century?

It so happens that no hockey player has ever suffered more from illegal tactics than Maurice Richard. He is a type of player few English-speaking Canadians understand. He is that rare thing, a champion who is also an obsessed artist. Latin that he is, he might easily have been a great matador had he been born in Spain. He has the courage, the grace, the intensity, the somber dignity. When you talk to him you feel he is as old as the hills and at the same time as young as a fresh-cheeked boy. Gentleness and ferocity both live in him. Even in a crowd he is strangely solitary. His eyes seem far away, and in hockey he has found a kind of personal destiny.

The reason he explodes is that he has again and again been prevented from playing hockey as well as he can because the referees have not enforced the rules properly. Every great player must expect to be marked closely, but for ten years the Rocket has been systematically heckled by rival coaches who know intuitively that nobody can more easily be taken advantage of than a genius. Richard can stand any amount of roughness that comes naturally with the game, but after a night in which he has been cynically tripped, slashed, held, boarded and verbally insulted by lesser men he is apt to go wild. His rage is curiously impersonal – an explosion against frustration itself.

It is bad for Richard and bad for the game that this kind of emotion has grown up around him, for it spreads far beyond the hockey rinks. Richard has become more than a hero to millions of *Canadiens*. Owing to the way in which he has been (so they think) persecuted, he has imperceptibly become the focus of the persecution-anxieties latent in a minority people. Not even the fact that he is loved and admired almost equally by English-speaking Montrealers can modify the profound self-identification of loyal *Canadiens* with this singular man.

They see in Richard not only a person who ideally embodies the fire and style of their race; they also see in him a man who from time to time turns on his persecutors and annihilates them.

It sounds fantastic to say it, but at the moment Richard has a status with some people in Quebec not much below that of a tribal god, and I doubt if even he realizes how much he stands for in the public mind is only indirectly connected with the game he plays.

First, a players'-eye view:

Jean Béliveau: *"On Sunday, March 13, we were in Boston, getting whipped 4-2 by the Bruins,"* he said. *"The score was not sitting well with us, because we were involved in a close race with Detroit for first place, and a loss to the fourth-place Bruins would be frustrating in the extreme. Late in the game, I faced off with Olmstead and Richard on my wings, and we moved down the ice. Maurice closed in on Hal Laycoe at the blue line, and it just so happened that Laycoe got his stick up and cut him. I was standing only a few feet away, and saw Maurice take his glove off. He passed his hand over the cut, and it came away covered with blood.*

"Maurice immediately went after Laycoe, and everybody else on the ice dropped their gloves and paired off. I took Fleming Mackell up against the glass and tried to follow the growing melee out of the corner of my eye."

Teammate Bernard Geoffrion tells it a little differently: *"It all started with a typical Richard rush. He barreled down the right side with the puck and was preparing for his patent left-turn swerve (button-hook) toward the Boston net. There was only one player in his way. Boston defenceman Hal Laycoe was tall, wore glasses and had once played with us in Montreal."* (He'd been the Rocket's tennis partner in the summer.)

"As Rocket went around him, Laycoe grabbed him by the waist and held on. Rocket carried him all the way to the corner where Laycoe gave him an elbow to the back of the neck and threw him into the chicken wire at the end of the rink.

AUTOGRAPH SESSION

Maurice Richard attracts a large crowd at a Quebec City toy store.

"Rocket was fuming. He turned around and swung his stick, just missing Laycoe. A second later, Laycoe swung his stick and hit Rocket for eight stitches in his scalp. The Rocket swung again and all of a sudden both benches emptied and every player from both teams was on the ice."

The Rocket was held back several times by linesman Cliff Thompson, but each time, either solely or with the help of a teammate, he managed to get free. For one final time, Thompson grabbed Richard and held him down on the ice. This time when the Rocket shrugged free, he turned around and punched Thompson in the face. Twice.

What is rarely reported is that Thompson, a Winchester, Mass., native in his rookie year as a linesman, was himself a former Bruins' defenceman. He had played for the Boston Olympics in the Eastern Hockey League and when the team moved into the Quebec Senior Hockey League, for more than a decade, and had played a dozen games with the NHL Bruins on both sides of military service in the Second World War.

It was common practice in the league then that linesmen be recruited locally from the ranks of former players (Aurel Joliat served in Montreal). Was Thompson more predisposed to gravitate toward a visiting player when a Bruin was threatened? That question would never be asked in the official inquiry conducted by Clarence Campbell, league president. Whether it matters, or not, Thompson would be gone after that season, never to officiate again in the NHL.

Richard was assessed a match penalty. Laycoe received a major penalty, and later a misconduct for not retiring to the penalty box in good time.

1955 Season Facts...

January 15 Maurice Richard plays in his milestone 700th career NHL game, and scores two goals in a 4-3 Canadiens loss to the Red Wings.
February 6 Richard scores four goals (for his twenty-fourth career hat trick) and adds an assist to lead the Canadiens to a 7-3 win against the Rangers, at New York.

The Richard Riot

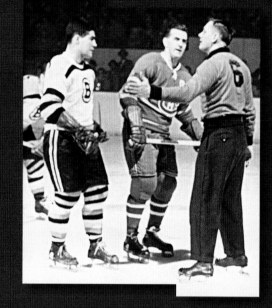

Maurice was increasingly involved with adversaries and officials like Red Storey (left) *and Frank Udvari* (top).

The Officials

You loved him, or you didn't, as fans, teammates, opponents, National Hockey League executives and, yes, even as officials.

The most compleat competitor of his era, it was pre-ordained that the Rocket would have run-ins with most of the league's officials.

On March 13, 1951, he was fined $500 for attacking referee Hugh McLean in the lobby of a Manhattan hotel. The previous evening, Richard had been assessed a game misconduct for fighting in the Forum penalty box with Detroit's Leo Reise, and later striking linesman Ed Mepham with his stick. When the Canadiens arrived at their New York hotel, the same officiating crew was in the lobby and three teammates had to pull the Rocket off the referee.

In December 1954, he was fined $250 for a brawl at Maple Leaf Gardens with Toronto's Bob Bailey, and struck linesman George Hayes in the face with his glove when the latter attempted to intervene.

And, of course, there was the infamous melee in Boston involving linesman Cliff Thompson and referee **Frank Udvari** that would lead to the Richard Riot.

Bill Chadwick and Red Storey were two of the league's most prominent arbiters during the Richard era, and their opinions diverged. Chadwick adopted an adversarial position with Richard, while Storey usually looked upon the Rocket with a more indulgent eye.

"Richard and Detroit's Ted Lindsay gave me the toughest time, although I never thought they were picking just on me," said Chadwick. *"It was because of their personal make-up and their character – they would have done it to anybody. Because of the way they were on the ice, I had a special thing I'd do with them at the start of every season.*

"In the first three or four games of every season, I'd give Richard and Lindsay misconduct penalties. I'd do it right away, because if I didn't they might think I wasn't the boss.

"Richard was perhaps the fiercest competitor I've ever seen in any sport. If you weren't playing on the same team with Maurice Richard, you were his enemy; and that applied if you were a referee giving him penalties."

The Rocket got his revenge many years later at a Lester Patrick Award function in New York. Chadwick, on the dais with the retired star and several other NHL names, asked him for an autograph for his son. Richard steadfastly refused.

Rocket didn't hate all of the officials, all of the time. He could be quite civil to Red Storey, for example.

"There was nothing funny about the Rocket when he was playing," Storey said. *"He was born to do one thing, and that was to score goals. Because of the trouble he kept getting into, most people thought the Rocket was hard to handle. I don't buy that, and I knew him pretty well in those days. His coaches never had any difficulty with him, nor did his teammates."*

Because he was (a) the game's best goal scorer and (b) had a hot temper, Richard was afforded close defensive attention, much of it outside the boundaries of the rules, some of that an effort to draw him into retaliation penalties. For as long as hockey has been played, the cliché has said: the instigator escapes; the retaliator is punished. Richard's reaction to what he considered acts outside the rules led to many of his suspensions and fines.

"No player in history was held or hooked or high-sticked the way he was," Storey added. *"He'd take it for as long as he could, but then watch out!"*

Needless to say, Boston was in an uproar the next day, with even the normally mild-mannered Bruins' president, Walter Brown, asking for a stiff rebuke for Richard. Boston columnist Pat Egan, who was the only journalist to take issue with Thompson's role in the affair, calling him a "hatchet man," was more understanding for a superstar who was the victim of cheap shots every time he ventured onto an NHL rink.

"Richard still has not learned to like or accept defeat. He is still ready to fight the world and I tell you that both for the good of hockey and the good of all sports that this man should be eligible for the playoffs," Egan wrote.

The affair was in the hands of Campbell, the former referee and lieutenant-colonel in the Canadian army, and member of the prosecutorial staff at the Nuremberg trials of Nazi war criminals. By the time of the Laycoe incident, he was not favorably predisposed to the Rocket.

In early 1954, a sports column by Maurice Richard titled *Le Tour du Chapeau* (Hat Trick), ghost written by a veteran Montreal sportswriter, regularly appeared in a Montreal weekly. In it, the Rocket savaged Quebec City fans for their poor treatment of his young brother, and then turned his guns on Campbell after Boom Boom Geoffrion was involved in a vicious stick-swinging duel with New York's Ron Murphy. The Rocket assailed the league president's handling of the affair, claiming that Geoffrion was over-penalized considering Murphy had started the affair, and then went on to accuse Campbell of anti-Canadiens' bias in several ways.

Richard will be suspended from all games, both league and playoff, for the balance of the current season.

– Clarence Campbell

He finished with: *"That is my frank opinion and if I am to be punished for it, well that's that. I will leave hockey and I have an idea that several other Canadiens players who share my opinion will do the same."*

Campbell read the riot act to Frank Selke and his assistant Ken Reardon, and was assured that Selke would handle the situation. Selke, who was as close to Richard as anyone in hockey, sat down with his star after a Chicago trip and, after a half-hour conversation, elicited the information that the Rocket had never written a word of the columns, but that he stood by them because his name was on them and he had given his word that he would. Rocket admitted several of his own opinions were faithfully represented in the columns, but he didn't necessarily agree with everything in them, especially the taunting of the league president.

Selke convinced Richard to withdraw from sports writing, and drafted a lengthy apology in Rocket's name. It was forwarded to the league, which promptly made it public, along with a $1,000 bond "to keep the peace." It immediately created a storm in the French media, which accused the NHL and Campbell of muzzling their hero.

It was a very rare Selke mistake in his days of managing the Canadiens, at least seen by a majority of Montrealers. The apology was too abject and smacked too much of a French underling kowtowing to an English boss, a common theme in east-end Montreal, and the Rocket's fans seethed for months.

On March 16, after convening all parties to NHL HQ, Campbell rendered his decision in a paper that resembled a legal document issued by the highest court in the land. Some 18 paragraphs outlining the events as they had been reported to him were written down. And then came the nineteenth paragraph: *"In the result, Richard will be suspended from all games, both league and playoff, for the balance of the current season."*

Maurice Richard and Kenny Reardon arrive for the hearing.

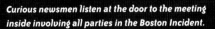
Curious newsmen listen at the door to the meeting inside involving all parties in the Boston Incident.

The fuse on the powder keg was lit; the explosion was imminent.

What made the situation so incendiary, of course, was the reaction by Hugh MacLennan's Two Solitudes. East of the Main, French Montreal was all righteous indignation and fury; West of the Main, most observers opined that the Rocket had been a loose cannon for years, and the league president had no choice but to tie him down. The media on both sides echoed those opinions faithfully:

La punition jugée trop forte — Too harsh a penalty (*La Presse*), with an underline, *Le maire Drapeau espère une révision du verdict* — Mayor Drapeau hoping for review of sentence. *Le Rocket ne jouera plus de la saison; Richard banni par Campbell* — Rocket won't play any more this season; Richard banished by Campbell (*Montréal-Matin*) and more in the French media, with the stories taking over the first page of the newspapers.

Reporter and columnist Jacques Beauchamp of *Montréal-Matin*, who served as a practice goalie for the Canadiens and who was one of two Montreal journalists in Boston on the fateful night (the other was Vince Lunny of *The Montreal Star*), had his story headlined: *Victime d'une nouvelle injustice, la pire celle-là, Maurice Richard ne jouera plus cette saison* — Victim of yet another injustice, the worst ever, Maurice Richard will play no more this season. A subhead asked: *"Had Campbell taken his decision before the meeting?"* Lunny's piece was just the opposite.

What added oil to the fire was that when he was suspended, Maurice Richard led the league in scoring with 74 points on 38 goals and 36 assists. Teammates Geoffrion (37-35 — 72 points) and Béliveau (36-35 — 71 points), were right behind him.

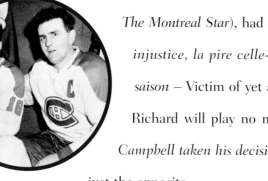

A Brother Act

October 15, 1955 *Montreal defeats the Rangers 4-1 at the Forum. Maurice Richard scores twice while his younger brother, Canadiens' rookie Henri, scores his first NHL goal.*

December 29, 1955 *Henri scores a goal and adds three assists, and the Rocket scores a goal and two assists to lead the Canadiens to a 5-2 win over the Maple Leafs, in Montreal. The goal is his 500th career NHL goal (including the playoffs).*

For all of his exploits, Maurice Richard had never won a scoring championship, and as a *La Presse* headline had trumpeted a week before the Boston incident, *"Maurice Richard is on the right road to realizing a great ambition."*

Both players idolized the Rocket, and were loath to take away this signal honor from him, but the team was in a championship race, with home-ice advantage against the defending champion Red Wings in the balance.

"This put me and the team in a bind," wrote Geoffrion. *"We had to win the remaining two games to finish first, which meant I had to play my best and try to score goals and set them up for my teammates. On the other hand, everyone wanted Rocket to win the scoring title especially now that he had been suspended for the rest of the season."*

Several teammates, including Béliveau and Harvey, convinced Geoffrion that he had to go all-out. Geoffrion passed Richard with a goal and two assists against the Rangers that night. The following night, the Red Wings clinched first place with a 6-0 whitewash of the visiting Canadiens.

Béliveau finished the story: *"A few days later, just before our first home game against Boston in the semi-finals, Maurice was introduced to the crowd, prompting a standing ovation that seemed as if it would never end. Minutes later, when Boom was presented with the Art Ross Trophy for winning the scoring race, the fans booed and littered the ice for almost as long as they had cheered the Rocket. Boom Boom remembered this episode for a long, long time."*

Drapeau vs. Campbell

Last, but not least, in the set-up for the events of St. Patrick's Day, was the war of words engaging prominent French Montrealers with their English counterparts, especially Campbell. Mayor Jean Drapeau raked the NHL president over the coals for his decision, and warned him to stay away from the game, claiming it would be seen by many as a "provocation."

In Ottawa, the Progressive Conservative Member for Trois-Rivières, Léon Balcer, attempted to bring up the issue as a "question of privilege" during the House of Common's Question Period, but was shouted down by the Liberal majority.

Rather than cowering Campbell, the electricity in the air seemed to stiffen his resolve. He was darned if he would bow down to the dregs of society. *"Does the Mayor suggest I should have yielded to the intimidation of a few hoodlums?"* Campbell said.

Maurice watched the first period of the Detroit game at rinkside.
ˇ

"What a strange and sorry commentary from the chief magistrate of our city who has sworn to uphold the law and as senior officer of the civic administration is responsible for the protection of the persons and property of the citizens through our police force.

"It is my right and my duty to be present at the game both as a citizen and as president of the league, and if the Mayor or Forum authorities have an apprehension they would not be able to deal with the situation and had requested me to absent myself, I would gladly have complied with their request. No such request was made or even suggested by anyone."

As game time approached, it was anything but business-as-usual at the Forum. Red Storey was the referee for the Detroit game.

"I realized just how serious it was when I got to the Forum maybe an hour before the game, and a crowd was already surrounding the building, chanting and yelling," Storey recalled. *"I got inside with no trouble, but someone came to our room about 15 minutes before game time and told us he'd had to hold his coat over his head to get into the Forum. The people were throwing bottles at the building and the glass was falling down on the sidewalk and the street. But I didn't get the feeling we might be in a bad situation until I went out on the ice. It was like being in a vacuum that was going to blow apart. It was so quiet it was scary."*

Campbell appeared midway through the period, occasioning a shower of tomatoes and other projectiles, and the tension rose when a young man wearing a leather jacket, André Robinson, 26, approached Campbell and punched him twice, or three times, depending on the report.

Fans mill in the street.

An assessment of damage
in the cold light of day.

As luck would have it, author Hugh MacLennan was sitting a couple rows in front of Campbell. He would write later, in *Saturday Night* magazine, that *"to understand the feelings of the crowd that night is to understand a good bit of the social conditions of Quebec in the 1950s. I remember knowing with very frightening and distinct certainty that with the mood of the mob, anything could happen."*

At period's end, the teams and game officials filed back to their dressing rooms. As they did, a tear-gas canister exploded a section over from where Campbell was sitting, filling the building with acrid fumes and sending everyone, police, firemen and paying customers, flooding to the exits. When this human tsunami hit the outside doors, it ran into an angry mob of 10,000 or so, triggering a surge eastward down St. Catherine Street.

City officials were powerless to contain the crowd as it transformed into a mob and began tearing up the city, destroying storefronts, looting stores, setting fires and overturning police cars. The mob would lay waste to most of the west-end downtown, and the city would not settle down until the next day.

Things were still bad at the Forum, where Storey was a reluctant participant in a very troubling incident.

"They'd ordered the building cleared. Once I heard that I went out into the hall to look for my wife, Helen. I mean, to hell with anything else. There was a riot going on. I couldn't find her and tried to ask a guy standing there, but he was yelling in French and I didn't understand him. Bill Roberts, a French Canadian despite his name, literally pushed me back into the dressing room. I was frantic, telling him I had to look for my wife, and he said: 'Look, you stupid bugger. He's telling you he's going to shoot you. He's a cop on duty and he's a little trigger happy.'"

"I didn't deserve a suspension that severe. I blame the linesman,
because he persisted in provoking me.

— Maurice Richard

The chief of police was summoned and the belligerent plainclothesman
was calmed down and put into a taxi for home. That's how hot emotions ran
in Montreal that night.

Maurice Richard spoke on radio to Montreal the next day, addressing his
fellow citizens in French and English, and all trouble ceased immediately.

As predicted by Montreal's French media, the Red Wings defeated the
Richard-less Canadiens in Detroit on April 14, 3-1, winning the Stanley Cup
final in seven games. To a man, woman and child, Montreal fans knew in their
hearts that the Rocket, the best playoff scorer the game had ever seen, would
have made a large contribution in reversing that result.

Clarence Campbell would never again sit comfortably in his Forum seats;
no matter how many Stanley Cups the Canadiens would win in ensuing years.

Dick Irvin would pay for the Boston Incident by losing his job of 15 years.

Fire and Oil

As a gritty player in the Patrick brothers' Pacific Coast Hockey Association with Portland Rosebuds, Dick Irvin often had clashes with the opposition "tough guys," and that approach carried over to his coaching career in aggressive, hard-driving teams. Of course, the intense, detest-your-foe Rocket Richard was an Irvin favorite in the 13 seasons they shared with the Canadiens.

Instead of placing tight restraints on the volatile Richard, Irvin often fed the Rocket's temper to spur him to greater heights as a player.

"Dick knew just the right word to make Maurice boil, sometimes going a bit too far, like trying to put out a fire with gasoline," said Toe Blake, Richard's long-time linemate who replaced Irvin as the Canadiens coach in 1955. *"I tried to handle Maurice different, keeping him cool and telling him that he didn't have to get even right away for every foul against him."*

Goalie Jacques Plante remembered Irvin as a "great" coach but not a man who handed out praise, once dressing down Plante after a 5-1 win because he had given up a soft goal.

"He came from a school of very hard hockey and that's how he coached," Plante said. *"But I think a pat on the back occasionally from Irvin would have helped everyone. One year (1951), the Rocket scored overtime goals to win the first two games of a semi-final in Detroit. We lost the next two at home and on the train back to Detroit, Dick called every player into his compartment and ate them out about it. The Rocket was really angry, saying 'I almost punched that grey-haired blankety-blank.'"*

Obviously, it worked. The Rocket had a goal in each of the next two games as Canadiens won the series.

A year later, after the Red Wings beat the Canadiens in the final, Irvin refused to shake hands with the champions, going immediately to the dressing room with Richard and Elmer Lach in his wake.

The Rocket's stormy 1954-55 season cost Irvin the coaching job. In a late December match-up at Toronto, Richard was in a scrap with Leafs rookie Bob Bailey, When the fight was settled, Richard skated to the Canadiens' bench, Irvin said something to him and the Rocket not only fought Bailey again, but clouted linesman George Hayes in the face with a glove.

Later in the season, Richard earned the suspension that inspired the St. Patrick's Day riot for a lengthy fight with the Bruins Hal Laycoe and a punch to linesman Cliff Thompson. Some Canadiens players said later that one of the four different sticks the Rocket used in the battle was handed to him by Irvin.

When the Canadiens, minus Richard, lost a seven-game final to the Red Wings, general manager Frank Selke fired Irvin as coach, claiming he had lost control of the players.

The fact that the Canadiens, especially the Rocket, looked upon ice officials as enemies, started with Irvin. When referee Red Storey was flattened by a player in a collision near the Canadiens bench and was prone on the ice, Irvin, the compleat needler, leaned over the boards toward Storey and said: *"Hope it's nothing trivial."*

More than three decades later, Maurice Richard was still bitter about the suspension costing him an Art Ross Trophy and, far more importantly, his team an opportunity of winning the Stanley Cup.

"I didn't deserve a suspension that severe," he said. *"I blame the linesman, because he persisted in provoking me. One thing most people don't know is that the league fired him after the season. But that doesn't help me or the Canadiens, eh?"*

The last word belongs to the late, great Québécois actor, Jean Duceppe, a cultural icon in his own right, who was interviewed by the National Film Board several years after the fact.

"The riot came about because the Richard suspension constituted an insult to the entire French-Canadian nation. You can try to minimize the whole affair, but the fact of the matter was that the entire French-Canadian nation had been 'reached' via Richard.

"The Riot; that's what it was all about."

The Rocket never forgave Clarence Campbell for his decision, although he was civil to the NHL President in subsequent years.
∨

FIRE ON THE ICE

By Herbert Warren Wind

December 6, 1954

Herbert Warren Wind was the Thinking Man's sports writer. Before applying fingers to keyboard, the graduate of Yale and Cambridge would amass prodigious amounts of research, approach the question at hand from all angles, and then produce a piece that was the envy of his peers.

He applied the Wind Scientific Method of Sports Writing to the columns and stories he wrote for 44 years in The New Yorker *and other publications and the world of sports literature.*

He joined The New Yorker *in the early 1950s and began his golf writing career with a piece on the immortal Robert Jones. He left that magazine in 1954 to help launch* Sports Illustrated, *returning to* The New Yorker *in 1960. He wrote two major pieces on the Canadiens, this one in 1954 in* Sports Illustrated, *and another 29-page piece in* The New Yorker *in 1979.*

During his career, both the PGA of America and the United States Golf Association awarded him their highest honors for golf reporting.

For all that has been said and written about the heights of fanatic devotion achieved by the fans of the Brooklyn Dodgers, the Notre Dame football teams and the Australian Davis Cup defenders, it is doubtful if there is any group of sports addicts anywhere which year in and year out supports its team with quite the supercharged emotion and lavish pride expended so prodigally by the citizens of bilingual Montreal on their hockey team, Les Canadiens – the Canadians. In June each year, four months before the next season begins, every seat in the Montreal Forum, save 800 or so that the management holds for sale on the day of the game, has been sold out for the entire 70-game schedule. On play-off nights it is not uncommon for crowds seeking standing-room to run into several thousands and to swarm over St. Catherine Street and beyond, into Atwater Park.

Hockey is deep in the Montrealer's blood. After a fine day by a member of the home team or, for that matter, of the visiting team, the Forum reverberates from the rink side to the rafters with sharp enthusiastic applause. But many volts above this in feeling and many decibels above in volume is the singular and sudden pandemonium that shatters the Forum, like thunder and lightning, whenever the incomparable star of Les Canadiens, Maurice (The Rocket) Richard, fights his way through the enemy defense and blasts the puck past the goalie. There is no sound quite like it in the whole world of sport.

A powerfully built athlete of 33 who stands five-ten and now weighs 180, having put on about a pound a year since breaking in with Les Canadiens in 1942, Joseph Henri Maurice (pronounced Mohr-riz, with the accent about equally divided) Richard (Ree-shar'), Gallicly handsome and eternally intense, is generally regarded by most *aficionados*, be they Montrealers or *étrangers*, as the greatest player in the history of hockey.

Flip through the pages of the record book; Most Goals – 384, set by Maurice Richard in 12 seasons (with the next man, Nels Stewart, a full 60 goals away); Most Goals in One Season – 50, set by Maurice Richard in a 50-game schedule in 1944-45; Most Goals in a Play-off Series – 12, Maurice Richard; Most Goals in a Playoff Game 5, Maurice Richard; Longest Consecutive Scoring Streak – at least one goal in nine consecutive games.

It is not simply the multiplicity of Richard's goals nor their timeliness but, rather, the chronically spectacular manner in which he scores them that had made the fiery right-winger the acknowledged Babe Ruth of hockey. *"There are goals and there are Richard goals,"* Dick Irvin, the old "Silver Fox" who has coached the Canadiens the length of Richard's career remarked not long ago. *"He doesn't get lucky now. Of these, 370 have had a flair. He can get to a puck and do things to it quicker than any man I've ever seen – even if he has to lug two defensemen with him, and he frequently had to. And his shots! They go in with such velocity that the net and all bulges."*

THE SEIBERT GOAL

One of the popular indoor pastimes year-round in Montreal is talking over old Richard goals – which one you thought was the most neatly set up, which one stirred you the most, etc., much in the way Americans used to hot stove about Ruth's home runs and do today about Willie Mays' various catches. In Irvin's opinion – and Hector (Toe) Blake and Elmer Lach, Richard's teammates on the famous Punch Line also feel this way – the Rocket's most sensational goal was "the Seibert goal," in the 1945-46 season. Earl Seibert, a strapping 225-pound defenseman who was playing for Detroit that season, hurled himself at Richard as he swept on a solo into the Detroit zone. The two collided with a thud, and as they straightened up, there was Richard, still on his feet, still controlling the puck, and sitting on top of his shoulders, the burly Seibert.

Richard not only carried Seibert with him on the way to the net, a *tour de force* in itself, but with that tremendous extra effort of which he is capable, faked the goalie out of position and with his one free hand somehow managed to hoist the puck into the far corner of the cage.

There is no question that Richard's most heroic winning goal was "the Boston goal" – the one he scored against the Bruins three years ago to lift Montreal into the finals of the Stanley Cup playoffs. *(See The Goal, page 70)*

For 10 years now because of his courage, his skill, and that magical uncultivatable quality, true magnetism, Maurice Richard has reigned in Montreal and throughout the province of Quebec as a hero whose hold on the public has no parallel in sport today unless it be the country-wide adoration that the people of Spain have from time to time heaped on their rare master matadors. The fact that 75% of the citizens of Montreal and a similar percentage of the Forum regulars are warm-blooded, excitable French-Canadians – and what is more, a hero-hungry people who think of themselves not as the majority group in their province but as the minority group in Canada – goes quite a distance in explaining their idolatry of Richard. *"If Maurice were an English-Canadian or a Scottish-Canadian or a kid from the West he would be lionized, but not as much as he is now,"* an English-Canadian Richard follower declared last month. *"I go to all the games with a French-Canadian friend of mine, a fellow named Roger Ouelette. I know exactly what Roger thinks. He accepts the*

English as good as anyone. But he would hate to see the French population lose their language and their heritage generally. He doesn't like that fact that the government's pension checks are printed only in English. He feels that they should be printed in both English and French since the constitution of the Dominion provides for a two-language country." For Roger, Maurice Richard personifies French Canada and all that is great about it. Maybe you have to have French blood, really, to worship Richard, but you know, you only have to be a lover of hockey to admire him.

And what about Le Rocket? How does he react to this fantastic adulation? Perhaps the surest key is the way he conducts himself after he scores one of his roof-raising goals. Down on the ice, below the tumult of tribute, Richard, while the referee is waiting for the clamor to subside before dropping the puck for the next face-off, cruises solemnly in slow circles, somewhat embarrassed by the strength of the ovation, his normally expressive dark eyes fixed expressionless on the ice. In his actions there is never the suspicion of the idol recognizing the plaudits of his fans. The slow circles which Richard transcribes after he has scored serve a distance purpose for him. They add up to a brief moment of uncoiling, one of the few he is able to allow himself during the six-months-long season. *"Maurice,"* Toe Blake once remarked, *"lives to score goals."* It is not that Richard puts himself above his team or the game. Quite the contrary, in fact. But here – and he has never been any other way – is a terribly intense man who, like so many of the champions who have endured as champions,

is forever driving himself to come up to the almost impossible high standard of performance he sets, whose pride in himself will not let him relax until he has delivered decisively and who, additionally, regards the veneration that has come his way as nothing less than a public trust that he must never let down. When Richard or Les Canadiens lose or when he is in the throes of a prolonged scoring slump, the Rocket will brood silently, sometimes for days at a time, limiting his conversations with his wife to "pass the butter" or "more water." Success affects Richard no less deeply.

STOPPING THE ROCKET

Because of his own scoring proclivities, Richard has for a dozen years been subjected to far more physical punishment than any other player since the National Hockey League was organized back in 1917. To beat Montreal, you must stop the Rocket, and to stop him opposing teams assign one man and sometimes two to do nothing but stay with Richard "right into the dressing room" if necessary. Some of the men assigned to Richard play him cleanly but, more often than not, opposing "defensive specialists" resort to

holding him, grabbing his jersey, hooking him, and whenever they get any kind of shot at him, belting him with their Sunday body check. One of the best ways to stop Richard, of course, is to get him off the ice. With this in mind, some of the rival teams have made it a practice to use a left wing against him with instructions to ignite deliberately the Rocket's red glare. Then, if Richard retaliates and the referee calls a double penalty, Montreal loses Richard and the other team a far less valuable man. Considering the abuse both physical and verbal he has taken from lesser men, Richard, all in all, has done a very good job of keeping his trigger temper under control, in recent years particularly. However, if he always ranks near the top in goals, he also does in penalty time, and not all of his penalties, by any manner of means, are the result of self protection. The Rocket probably holds the league record for misconduct penalties, 10-minutes "rests" which are awarded for telling the referees off in overly pungent language. And the Rocket is always up among the leaders, for that matter, in major penalties, five-minute cool-off sessions for fighting. He has lost some fights, but only when he has been ganged up on. In man-to-man combat, he acquits himself extremely well. When Bill Juzda of the Leafs challenged him one night, Maurice stripped off his gloves and flattened Juzda with one blow. In 1945 he knocked down Bob (Killer) Dill of the Rangers twice on the ice, and when Dill decided to start things again in the penalty box Richard knocked him out.

LA REVUE SPORTIVE du *Forum* SPORTS MAGAZINE

25¢

Maurice Richard

1958-59 CINQUANTENAIRE - GOLDEN ANNIVERSAR

WINDING DOWN

$\mathcal{M}$aurice Richard began the winding-down phase of his illustrious career by stepping up – all the way to captain of the Montreal Canadiens at 35 years of age. In the first six seasons of the Rocket's NHL days, Toe Blake wore the C, sharing the captaincy in the 1947-48 season with goalie Bill Durnan, the last time a netminder was allowed to be a team captain. When Blake left the NHL in 1948, defenceman Emile *Butch* Bouchard took up the post and held it until he retired after the 1956 Stanley Cup championship. Richard was the obvious choice to replace him as captain. **9**

"From about his third season with the Canadiens, Maurice was the club inspiration, the leader with his own drive and intensity, which rubbed off on the other players without him giving pep talks or saying much of anything," Blake said long after he retired as coach in 1968.

"A big part of the captain's job for me, and then Butch, for a long time was trying to keep Maurice on an even keel. That wasn't always an easy task."

The 1955-56 season was to be the last time the Rocket played a full schedule of 70 games. He scored 38 goals, finishing third in the scoring race behind Jean Béliveau and Gordie Howe. In the Stanley Cup playoffs, when the Canadiens began their incredible run of five consecutive triumphs, Richard was vintage Rocket with 14 points in 10 games as the Canadiens eliminated the New York Rangers and arch-rival Detroit in a pair of five-game affairs.

The string of increasingly serious injuries that dogged the late years of the Rocket's career began the following year, albeit with a minor wound. Richard missed seven games early in the schedule when surgery was required to remove bone chips from his elbow. But he did score 33 goals in 63 games and demonstrated several times that age had not banked his competitive fires.

From his third season with the Canadiens, Maurice was the club inspiration, the leader with his own drive and intensity.

– Toe Blake

To the day he retired as a player, Richard never abandoned the idea that the officials employed two sets of rules where he was concerned. One group of arbiters allowed opponents much leeway in fouls against him while the hockey laws applied to him were much stricter. He even hinted occasionally that being French Canadian meant different treatment from the referees.

In a January, 1957 game at the Forum against the Maple Leafs, referee Frank Udvari, perceived as a Canadiens' nemesis, gave the Rocket a high-sticking penalty that Richard felt was undeserved. He protested mildly to Udvari while the fans threw objects on the ice. When the Leafs tied the game on the power play, Richard's ire level soared, and he argued vehemently with Udvari as he emerged from the penalty box. When it appeared he might strike the official, his mates quickly restrained their captain while the fans covered the ice with hats, rubbers, drink cups and programs.

The crowd started to jeer NHL president Clarence Campbell, who was at the game, and, for a brief moment, there was fear of a repeat of the 1955 St. Patrick's Day riot. Udvari needed a police escort off the ice at the game's conclusion.

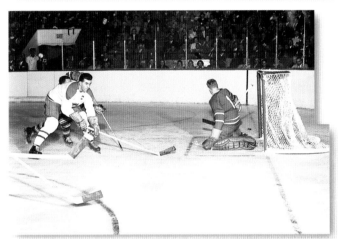

^
This is how it's done...
the Rocket blasts in and scores
on Toronto's Johnny Bower.

^
*February 28, 1958:
the Canadiens clinch
first place with a lot of
schedule remaining.*

HOCKEY'S HIGH FLYERS

*Air turbulence is the order of the day
when a Rocket meets a Cyclone (Fred
Taylor) at the Hockey Hall of Fame.*

With injuries a large factor, the Canadiens finished second, six points behind the Red Wings, and two in front of the improved Boston Bruins. But when the playoffs started, the Canadiens' new captain was not about to allow any derailment of the club's run.

Richard scored in four of the five games as the Canadiens eliminated the Rangers, including an overtime goal in the series' clinching game. In the opener of the final against the Bruins, Richard scored four times to start the Canadiens on a five-game romp to the Cup.

The Rocket actually smiled during his first acceptance of the NHL's top trophy as captain from his long-time bitter enemy, president Campbell.

God Bless You, Johnny Quilty

During his year with the Verdun Maple Leaf juniors (1940-41), Maurice Richard had the opportunity to practise occasionally at The Forum, and it was here that an incident that would mark him for life took place one afternoon.

The junior Leafs had finished their workout and were leaving the rink as the NHL Canadiens straggled in for their own practice later in the day. The Rocket was at the players' entrance when he noted the arrival of **Johnny Quilty**, the Ottawa native who would win the Calder Trophy as the league's Rookie of the Year that season.

Maurice thrust a paper and pen in front of the young sensation, a graduate of the Ottawa St. Patricks, who was a scant seven months older than him.

He was rebuffed. *"I don't sign autographs,"* Quilty said. *"I didn't speak much English at the time, but I remembered those words,"* the Rocket said a half century later.

For his entire career, and post-career, Maurice Richard would meticulously handle all autograph requests, some times numbering in the hundreds. He took his time too, carefully signing an autograph that was clear and legible.

"If they are going to honor me by asking for my autograph, it must mean something to them," he said. *"The least I can do is leave no doubt that it is my autograph."*

Johnny Quilty played two full seasons with Montreal before signing up for military service in 1942. When he returned to the Canadiens in 1946-47, he would play another twenty-nine regular season games and seven playoff contests with Montreal and Boston before resuming his career in senior hockey. His NHL line reads: 125 regular season and 13 playoff games played, a total 39 goals scored and 39 assists for 78 career points.

The autograph seeker at the Forum that day did a little better in pro hockey.

Late Career Injuries

Maurice receives a magnificent forged iron lamp from the Montreal Technical Institute – where he once was a student – to honor his 500th NHL goal.

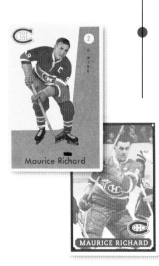

As captain of an exceptional team, Richard started the 1957-58 season on a high note, scoring the 500th goal of his career, six games into the schedule. Then came a low point in his career. In a November 13 game against the Maple Leafs, the Rocket fell when struck by a shot and the skate of Leafs defenceman Marc Réaume severed the Achilles tendon just above his right heel. There was talk that the Rocket's career might be over.

But he was skating lightly in late January and, on February 20, the Forum was packed for the Rocket's return after a 42-game absence, which, of course, was dramatic. He played a full shift on a line with brother Henri and Dickie Moore and scored two picture goals against Boston.

Moore and Pocket Rocket finished one-two in scoring as the Canadiens finished first, 19 points in front of the Rangers. They played third-place Detroit in the semi-final, a series that added another chapter to the Rocket legend.

Richard scored two goals in each of the first two games, easy wins for the Canadiens, who also won the third game in overtime. In the fourth game at the Detroit Olympia, the Red Wings led, 3-1, after the second period.

"In our dressing room before the third period, we were all feeling very frustrated because the Wings were playing well," said goalie Jacques Plante. *"No one said it but we seemed to be thinking that it was their night, and we would have to get them next game.*

"When it came time to go on the ice for the third period, the Rocket leaped to his feet like he had been shot out of a cannon and said, almost with a growl: 'They got three goals so why can't we?' He had done something like that so seldom that the fire in his eyes was like a lightning bolt to the team."

The Rocket scored twice, giving him three for the game, and Moore added a single as the Canadiens rebounded for a 4-3 win and a sweep of the series.

That sent the Canadiens against the Bruins in the final and after the teams split the first two games in Montreal, the Rocket scored twice in a 3-0, third-game win at Boston. The Bruins evened the series again before the sixth overtime goal of Richard's career won the fifth game and he added another in a 5-3 Cup-winning victory.

At 37, Richard led all playoff shooters with 11 goals in 10 games, really the last big hurrah of his career. Wounds and weight would take a toll in his last two seasons.

April 21, 1958
It's a family affair at Windsor Station as the Canadiens return from Boston and a third straight Stanley Cup victory.
∨

The 1958-59 season was another discouraging one for the Rocket, who had scored 17 goals and 38 points in 42 games when he fell into the boards in Chicago in a mid-January game.

"I felt something snap and I had broken enough bones in my life to know I was in trouble," said Richard, who had a broken bone in his ankle.

The Rocket did not play again during the schedule. He missed the entire semi-final against the Blackhawks, which the Canadiens won in six games. Richard dressed for the opener of the Cup final against the Maple Leafs, but took only a few shifts in the four games of the series he played, Canadiens winning in five games. With Moore, Marcel Bonin and Bernie Geoffrion in high gear, Richard shared in the fourth consecutive Cup triumph for the team, but it was the first time he had failed to score a goal in 15 years of playoffs.

ALL-STAR BROTHER ACT

October 4, 1958 *Maurice Richard scores twice and brother Henri has the game winner and two assists, as the Stanley Cup Champions defeat the NHL All-Stars 6-3. Dickie Moore assists on all three Richard brothers' goals, an all-star record for 30 years.*

When the Rocket scored only three goals in the first 11 games of the 1959-60 season, there was talk that he was out of shape and slowing down. But he showed that the competitive fires still burned when he belted the Bruins big winger John Bucyk into the boards, and Bucyk went to the hospital with shoulder and knee injuries.

I felt something snap,
and I had broken enough bones in my life
to know I was in trouble.

– Maurice Richard

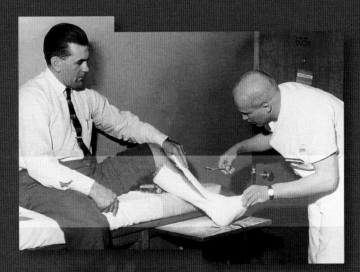

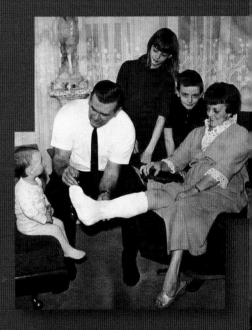

For once, the cast is on the other foot, as Lucille Richard shows off hers to husband and children.

The Last Game

The Stanley Cup sits on a small table at centre ice of Maple Leaf Gardens in Toronto and standing beside it is the Rocket, microphone in his left hand, his right clasped in a handshake with NHL President Clarence Campbell, his long-time nemesis. Both men wear broad smiles.

The Canadiens have just defeated the Toronto Maple Leafs, 4-0, to complete a sweep (eight games) of the 1960 playoffs and win the team's fifth consecutive Stanley Cup. It is the last National Hockey League game that Maurice Richard will ever play.

The Rocket was held scoreless in the game, but his brother Henri had a goal while two more legends, Jean Béliveau, with two, and Doug Harvey, scored the others for the champions.

When he skated off the Gardens ice that night, April 14, 1960, Richard's magnificent career was over, although the announcement of his retirement was still five months and a day away. The speculation was rampant throughout the playoffs as Richard played on a bad foot, showing little of the dramatic flair that was his trademark.

After 4-2 and 2-1 wins in Montreal to open the final, the series continued at Toronto's Maple Leaf Gardens, a building where the Rocket never felt comfortable and did not play his best. Canadiens coach Toe Blake once blamed a female fan seated close to the visitors' bench for the Rocket's ordinary record in MLG.

"She's an older lady with the foulest mouth I ever heard in a human, male or female," Blake said.

"Her favorite target was Maurice and she seemed to get under his skin with no trouble. Another thing was the clutching and grabbing tactics the Leafs always used against him."

The easy 5-2 victory in Game Three showed off the Canadiens' depth. Third-line centre Phil Goyette scored two goals and ace penalty killer Don Marshall added another. In the second period, Maurice accepted a pass from brother Henri and went to cut across the front of the Leafs' goal. His way was barred so he circled behind the net, emerging on the opposite post, and let a backhand go just as he made his turn. The puck found the net.

It would be the last goal he would ever score, number 626 combined and number 82 in playoffs.

Those attending the game may have sensed the significance of the gesture when Richard fished the puck out of Johnny Bower's goal. *"I regretted that I didn't keep the puck from my first playoff goal but, at least, I have the puck for my eighty-second. If I keep on playing and score more, I'll give this puck to some kid,"* Richard explained.

In spite of his foot problems, the right-winger took full shifts in the fourth game. He had two good scoring chances, forcing Bower to make a spectacular save on a close-in shot.

Years later, Richard recalled his good-bye match.

"It would have been nice to score a goal in the game that was to be my last," he said. *"But, I got to do the only thing that really mattered. I carried off the Stanley Cup that we had won one more time."*

The serious injury jinx still haunted the Rocket in the 1959-60 season. In a late November game, he was struck in the face by the puck and suffered a depressed fracture of the cheekbone. That cost him 19 games, but in early January he was playing again, finishing the season with a 19-16 – 35 point total in 51 games. Richard had a bothersome foot bruise in the playoffs when the Canadiens swept to the record fifth consecutive Stanley Cup championship, ousting the Blackhawks and Maple Leafs in a minimum of eight games, yielding only 11 goals.

The Rocket worked an irregular shift in the playoffs and scored a goal, in the third game, the final tally for the great shooter. The Cup-clinching fourth game was the Rocket's farewell match after 18 of the most illustrious, tempestuous and victorious seasons of any NHL player.

The following records were held or shared by Maurice Richard, at the time of his retirement from hockey:

CAREER

Most goals, regular season	**544**
Most goals, season and playoffs	**626**
Most points, regular season	**965**
Most points, season and playoffs	**1,091**
Most goals, playoffs	**82**
Most points, playoffs	**126**
Most consecutive 20-goal seasons	**14**
Most consecutive all-star team selections	**14**
Maximum games with three or more goals, season and playoffs	**33**
Longest series of goals in games	**14**
	(in 9 games)

OTHERS

Most winning goals	**101**
Most unassisted goals	**71**
Most two-goal games	**134**
Most four-goal games	**6**
Most five-goal games	**2**
Most first goals of a game	**120**

SEASON

Most goals in a season 1944-45	**50** (in 50 games)
Most points in a game	**8**

STANLEY CUP

Most overtime goals	**6**
Most game-winning goals	**18**
Most unassisted goals	**10**
Most two-goal games	**17**
Most three-goal games	**7**
Most four-goal games	**3**
Most five-goal games	**1**
Best goal-per-game average	**0.616**
Most points in one period	**4**
Most assists in one period	**3**
Longest consecutive scoring streak (twice)	**8**
Most goals in a playoff year 1943-44	**12** (in 9 games)
Most goals scored in a single playoff game (vs. Toronto, March 22, 1944)	**5**
Most assists in a single playoff game	**5**

The Last Scrimmage

Would the Rocket go or stay?

^
September 15, 1960, was a very sad day for Montreal sports fans.

In the summer of 1960 after the Canadiens' fifth consecutive Stanley Cup triumph, that question dominated many Montreal conversations.

"I couldn't go anywhere that summer without people asking if Maurice was leaving," said Toe Blake, the Canadiens coach and former linemate of the Montreal sniper. *"It was the same as an election: Is the Prime Minister going to win?"*

Carrying extra weight and a good tan from a summer of golfing and fishing, Richard did go to the Canadiens' training camp that September. In a scrimmage one morning, he scored four goals. And then the most scintillating career in the National Hockey League came to an abrupt end.

"His shot release never looked quicker than in that last scrimmage," said goalie Jacques Plante, who had seen a lot of Richard rubber in a decade of team practices. *"The players were telling him that he might be an 'old Rocket' but he was faster than any of the new ones. That's why what happened that day was a surprise."*

After the scrimmage, Richard went to Blake's office and told the coach he was retiring from the game. That summer, Frank Selke the team's managing director, told Richard that if he retired, the team would give him a public relations job and, for the first three years, he would receive his playing salary. Richard went from Blake's office to Selke's, and a press conference was called.

"There were very few more emotional gatherings than the Rocket's retirement announcement," said Andy O'Brien, who had covered the Canadian sports scene for close to 40 years.

"We all knew how difficult it was for Richard to leave something he loved as much as playing hockey. His voice was the most subdued I ever heard it, and many of the so-called, hard-boiled media people shed a few tears that day."

"I can never repay hockey for what it has done for me and my family," Richard said.

Years later, in reflecting on that day, Richard was of another opinion.

"I wasn't ready to retire in 1960," he said. *"I would have loved to keep going and I should have tried harder."*

Richard acknowledged a weight problem.

"In 1960, my playing weight was about 210 pounds and it hurt my play because I needed to be 25 pounds lighter. My reflexes weren't the same. I was slower and couldn't avoid the bodychecks the way I had. But as I got up into my 30s, I should have worked out and dieted all summer to be ready.

"In my last three seasons I had pretty bad injuries, and my wife was worried that I might get hurt seriously. I thought about that, too, but I should have done more to take care of myself."

Richard refuted any direct charge that Selke had pushed him into retirement before he was ready. However, when his relationship with the Canadiens organization soured in the late 1960s, he dropped hints that perhaps he should have followed his heart and played another season or more.

Frank Selke would have been the happiest hockey executive alive had Maurice Richard been able to extend his career.

"We haven't been able to replace him and maybe we never will. He was the most dedicated player I have ever seen in all the years I've been in hockey."

A SIMPLE FAMILY MAN

$\mathcal{M}$aurice Richard was truly a Lion in

Winter, ferocious on the ice in the face of

enemies and adversity, and the leader of his

pride, his family, at home. The Canadiens were

one family, the rapidly expanding and extended

Richard clan was his other, and he owed them

his loyalty and support at all times. ❾

Maurice Richard was Frank Selke's model, but not only for his skills on the ice. The managing director was a devout Roman Catholic whose beliefs in family values were deeply entrenched. He was impressed by the Rocket and his relationships with his family and the community.

"It was inevitable that I should get to know his wife (Lucille) well, and to respect her as a perfect mate for the moody and explosive Rocket," Selke said. *"It has often been said that a good wife is a man's most prized possession. Whenever I meet this young French-Canadian couple, I cannot help but feel that Canada could do with many more thousands of devoutly religious people like Maurice and Lucille Richard.*

"One of the first things that impressed me about Maurice Richard was his parents, Onésime and Alice, and the way they reared their children. Maurice was respectful, loyal, hard-working and independent of spirit, while being a staunch team man. I wanted more players with this kind of character especially those to whom playing for the Montreal Canadiens would be something special.

"The French-Canadian family was a special unit and I wanted to be able to recruit a lot of boys who had grown up with the same values the Rocket had. And it certainly would do the Canadiens right if we could rebuild the image of the Flying Frenchmen, because the zeal and temperament of Quebec boys made hockey their natural game."

Maurice Richard was part of the extended Quebec family, such was his popularity during his playing days. When brother Henri joined the team, the Richard family, in toto, was adopted by Canadiens' fans everywhere. For example, Mrs. Alice Richard was honored at the Garden by the Mayor of Boston on Valentine's Day, 1956, as Hockey Mother of the Year. The ceremony, part of a weekend safari to Boston, was attended by some 800 staunch Canadiens' fans from Montreal and Alice Richard held court in the stands. The local fans soon warmed up as well to the astonishingly at-ease mother of five sons and three daughters – among them the superstar, Maurice, and the rising star, Henri.

OCTOBER 6, 1960

Jacques Plante recorded his forty-eighth career shutout in the Canadiens 5-0 win over Toronto in Montreal. Before the game, Maurice Richard's uniform No. 9 was retired in a special ceremony.

The French-Canadian family was a special unit and I wanted to recruit boys who had grown up with the same values the Rocket had.

– Frank Selke

A Simple Family Man

121

Henri joining the Canadiens had made her life easier, Alice opined.

"Before that, with Maurice in the National Hockey League, Henri playing Junior A and Claude playing Junior B, sometimes I wished there were at least two of me to attend all the games!" Henri and Maurice played together on five Stanley Cup teams, but the biggest thrill for Mr. and Mrs. Onésime Richard came in an exhibition game at the Forum on Saturday, September 19, 1959.

The Canadiens were playing their senior league farm club, the Montreal Royals, and the spotlight was on the All-Richard Line. Maurice had just passed his thirty-eighth birthday, Henri was 23 and Claude was just under 22.

To the emotion-filled parents and fans it was a night from which dreams are built. But the Richard trio would never see regular NHL action together. Claude was assigned to the Montreal Royals in the Eastern Professional Hockey League and was still there when Maurice retired a year later.

Alice Richard spent her life in hockey arenas with three sons playing competitively.

> *Sometimes I wished there were at least two of me to attend all the games!*
>
> – Alice Richard

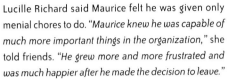

Rift with the Forum

^
Maurice Richard set up several home businesses, including one where he sold fishing line.

Frank Selke always claimed that he nudged Maurice Richard towards retirement in 1960 because of the serious injuries suffered in the three previous seasons and the noticeable loss of speed, always the Rocket's strong point. Selke was prominent among those who didn't want Richard to hang on in the league past his peak, diminishing what once had been sublime.

That's why the Canadiens managing director offered Richard a public relations job at his hockey salary for three years. The Rocket found the public relations job to be an exercise in futility.

"I never stopped thinking I should be helping the team," the Rocket said. *"That meant a hand in the hockey operations and decision-making side of things. Such an offer was never forthcoming.*

"I missed the excitement of the game and, yes, the attention it brought me. But, I felt I could seriously contribute off the ice, but I wasn't given the opportunity.

"I guess people still wanted to see me because I went to banquets, hockey tournaments, charity events, six or seven days a week, all year round. I went all over Canada and some spots in the United States, too. I spent no time with my wife and kids. It was no life."

After two years on the move, Richard told Selke that he wanted his schedule of appearances eased drastically. Selke agreed and told Richard his salary would stay the same. His load was reduced but, a year later, his pay was cut in half.

"I finished that year, then I quit the job altogether," Richard said. *"I went home a free man who could do what he wanted. It was one of the best days of my life out of hockey."*

The Rocket briefly tried a job as assistant to Canadiens president J. David Molson. The plan was for him to learn all sides of the team's operation, working in different departments. But that meant much time in the office and Richard could not last cooped up inside when he knew the fish were biting in northern Quebec.

Lucille Richard said Maurice felt he was given only menial chores to do. *"Maurice knew he was capable of much more important things in the organization,"* she told friends. *"He grew more and more frustrated and was much happier after he made the decision to leave."*

The Rocket found being a spectator a difficult chore, almost as enervating as playing a game. Twice, he felt opponents took liberties with Canadiens and tried to punch them from the seats when they headed for the dressing room at the end of periods.

"I still was thinking like a player and found watching games tougher than playing in them," Richard said. *"For a while, I only went to a few games and often left after a period or two."*

The split with the Canadiens lasted 18 years. Richard was not a rich man but he had enough money for his family to be comfortable. He bought a rundown tavern in downtown Montreal and renovated it, and renamed it Tavern Number Nine, spending a few hours there every day. He sold it three years later and doubled his investment.

The Rocket used the profits to buy a small fishing line company, which he operated out of his house for 23 years. He bought several types of line in bulk and at a table in his basement, wound the line onto spools, each carrying a small autograph, and marketed under the "Clipper" label. He travelled the province of Quebec, delivering the line to sporting goods stores and fishing camps.

He had several endorsements for cars, tea and hair dye plus promotional work for S. Albert, a fuel company, an association that lasted more than 40 years. *"I was in good shape financially with solid investments,"* he said. *"I only worked because I liked it."*

Richard played for the Montreal Oldtimers team until he was 57, then refereed the games, the only official more popular than the players. The games raised much money for charities in all parts of the country.

"In the summer I could go fishing whenever I felt like it and that turned out to be quite often," Richard said.

Maurice was given a hero's welcome in the Soviet Union and in Czechoslovakia, and thoroughly enjoyed his visits to Moscow and Prague.

European Trips

Maurice Richard once said that a big surprise of his life came when he discovered that he had many fans in Europe.

"When I went to Czechoslovakia and found out that people there had even heard of me, I was a little shocked," the Rocket said.

Richard made two trips to that country and was bestowed heroic status in a Communist nation that had no television at the time. But as hockey was moving out of its Canadian and, to a lesser degree, American shell, even behind the Iron Curtain the NHL was recognized as the top league in the world.

In 1959, Richard attended the world hockey championships in Prague and when he walked into the arena in that glorious old city for the first game in the tournament, more than 20,000 fans rose to their feet and chanted very loudly: *"Rock-et... Rock-et... Rocket."*

"That was a great surprise because the newspapers there did not even carry NHL standings," Richard said. *"One official told me that the newsreels in the movie theatres often had sports events in them. A few years earlier, someone had sent me a magazine from Moscow that had more than two million copies printed and there was a story about Henri and me in it."*

When he retired as a player in 1960, an early assignment as roving ambassador for the Canadiens was for Maurice and his wife Lucille to attend a summer sports festival in Prague. A large outdoor sports stadium full of fans greeted him warmly.

A 1967 trip to Europe that had no pre-departure publicity attracted considerable attention. For many years, retired professional players and senior amateurs played in the Montreal Depression Hockey League for conditioning and fun. That year, a team from the league, including Richard, made a trip to France to play against local teams.

A news agency reported the first game and readers of *The Gazette* saw a March 27 headline that said: *Rocket gets two goals in 6-2 win.* The Depression boys had beaten the French champion Chamonix to open the tour.

Again, Richard received a large reception. Posters carrying his picture were used to publicize the game at Grenoble, which would be the site of the 1968 Winter Olympic Games. Such a large crowd turned out that a second game was scheduled the next night to accommodate those who could not get into the arena.

The Rocket scored 18 goals in eight games played in 11 days and showed that he had not lost the stir-up-trouble touch. After the tour ended, the French Ice Hockey Federation suspended all players and even the referees in the games against the tourists for violating a rule that forbade amateurs to play against pros.

Dad First, Player Second

Whereas Maurice Richard was a surrogate father or Big Brother to many teammates, it was as *paterfamilias* of his own burgeoning clan that he excelled. He was a hockey playing version of Robert Young, star of the popular TV sitcom, *Father Knows Best*.

When Lucille Norchet was in hospital having one of the seven Richard children, the Rocket would camp out in the waiting room for the duration. And when the new son or daughter would arrive, the man who terrorized goaltenders all over North American would weep unashamedly.

Wife Lucille and her mother were interviewed by June Callwood for *Maclean's* magazine in the early 1950s. The subject was the domesticated Rocket. *"He's supposed to be so hard, but wait till you see him at home,"* said his wife.

"He's so gentle and kind, so good to the kids. Too good, I tell him."

Mrs. Norchet chimed in: *"Remember Huguette's ski pants?"*

"She wanted the stretchy kind, they cost $40," said Lucille. *"Maurice got mad and said it was crazy for a girl to have ski pants that cost $40. The next day he went and bought them himself."*

Maurice Richard spent most of his free time with his family.

Onésime and Maurice celebrate another milestone by the Rocket. Onésime was a solid athlete in his own right; a decent defenceman in hockey. The sport at which he excelled, however, was baseball, and he played it competitively into his 40s.

Mrs. Norchet: *"And when they're sick he almost drives Lucille crazy. He keeps asking her if they have their medicine, if it's the right kind, does the doctor know about it? Same when she isn't well. If she forgets to take her medicine, he is wild."*

Maurice Richard would not dispute the comments of wife and mother-in-law. He also admitted learning from the best father he had ever known, Onésime Richard, who espoused a parental philosophy of strictness and fairness.

'They can have anything they want, anything at all," said Maurice. *"I want them home or else I want to know where they are and whom they are with. That's the only rule. Rocket (junior) was going to a school where he hung around afterwards with the rest of the boys. I took him out and put him in another school. Now he comes home. And Huguette, she goes skiing on weekends and the priest is always with them. If the children are at home or with good people, they are not getting into trouble, that's for sure."*

By the late 1950s, most Canadians were familiar with the Richard clan: Huguette, Maurice Jr., Normand, André, Suzanne, Paul and Jean. On many a Saturday night, Lucille and one of the three eldest children (Huguette, Rocket Jr. and Normand), would attend the games at the Forum. *"People seldom noticed,"* laughed Lucille, *"but Maurice always waved his stick at us at the start of each period. Sometimes I think he did it to bring him luck, but it was affection, too."*

I want my kids home or else I want to know where they are and whom they are with.

That's the only rule.

– Maurice Richard

Rocket the Coach

From that day in July 1972 when he signed on as the first coach of the Quebec Nordiques in the new World Hockey Association, those who knew Maurice Richard called it a mistake.

That outlook was accurate. The Rocket's coaching career lasted only two games, and he had to be coaxed into handling the team in the second one. After the Nordiques had lost their season inaugural, 2-0, to the Crusaders in Cleveland, Richard resigned. But the club owners and management talked him into staying behind the bench for the team's home opener at Le Colisée.

Despite a 6-0 win over the Edmonton Oilers, Richard said he would take a week off to "think things over." He never returned.

The Nordiques had signed the Rocket and defence-man **Jean-Claude Tremblay** of the Canadiens to give the new team the appeal, for fans and players, of two big names in Quebec hockey.

But Richard's friends felt that his temperament was not suited to coaching, especially with a new, struggling team.

"Maurice had little use for teammates who did not have his intensity about helping the team win and would make any sacrifice to do it, and he quickly realized that he would have mostly minor leaguers to coach," said Jacques Plante, who would sign on as coach and general manager of the Nordiques in the team's second season (1973-74).

"But he always felt that the Canadiens should have given him a job more important than Goodwill Ambassador. He grabbed the first chance offered to him to show they were wrong and realized quickly that the job would give him only frustration.

"Maurice told me a few years later that he knew in his first years of training camp that he didn't have the patience or the tact for the job, so he stepped away as quickly as he could."

^
Coaching baseball and attending sports events for kids was more agreeable for Maurice Richard.

After retiring in 1960, Richard still managed to travel frequently, but would still phone home nightly to "check on the kids." One after another, they would troop to the telephone receiver to get their dollop of long-distance quizzing and fatherly concern. If they weren't at home, Dad would want to know about it the next night.

Maurice was also very involved with his sons' sporting interests, and was a regular at baseball fields and hockey arenas all over Quebec when the boys played. Quite often he would "father" a dozen or so other boys by coaching. Sometimes, the Richard name would backfire, and the Rocket would launch a defensive charge that was devastating in its force.

One such occasion occurred at Le Colisée in Quebec City when Rocket Jr. was playing for a Montreal team in the renowned Quebec peewee tournament. For some reason, Maurice Richard Jr. was copiously booed. The next day's newspapers were full of denunciations of the provincial capital by an enraged father. It was a tempest in a teapot, but the Rocket for years bad-mouthed Quebec City to anyone who would listen.

The Richard family was Quebec royalty, even though some Quebeckers were anti-monarchists. Occasionally, the Richards were called upon to meet august personages from all walks of life.

The couple who wedded as kids in 1942, hardly able to speak a word of English, would certainly have been left in a state of shock if futuristic television had flashed coverage of an evening to come about a decade later when "Mr. Hockey" and his wife were invited by Queen Elizabeth to dinner in Ottawa.

Andy O'Brien wrote of an amicable evening spent *à table*.

"No longer shy, but now proud of the national recognition given him as the greatest in the game he so loved, Maurice Richard later confessed he had become 'a little excited' and addressed Prince Philip by his first name.

" 'But he didn't seem to mind,' said Richard, 'in fact, he called me Maurice – or Rocket – I don't remember which.'

"And how about the Queen and Mrs. Richard?

" 'Oh, they talked about their children.'

STICK TO IT, GRANDPA

If Maurice was a proud papa, he became an even more attentive "grand-papa", doting on a third generation of Richards. Here, he and the grand-kids read about grandpa in a book extolling the Richardian trademark tenacity.

> **Maurice Richard later confessed he had become 'a little excited' and addressed Prince Philip by his first name.**

– Andy O'Brien

A Simple Family Man

CLOSING THE FORUM

*I*t was High Opera in Scarlet, equal parts

Aida, Requiem Mass and Viking Funeral,

with a Wagnerian air thrown in. It was a

funeral for a building, the Forum, Montreal's

most recognized stage and landmark. On this

Monday night, March 11, 1996, the Montreal

Canadiens had just defeated the Dallas Stars, 4-1,

some 71 years, three months and 29 days (Leap Year

Days factored in) after the *bleu-blanc-rouge* had opened

the Forum with a 7-1 win over Toronto. 9

On November 29, 1924, Billy Boucher scored 56 seconds into the game to inaugurate what would become the most famous hockey arena in the world. Billy was a member of the Ottawa Bouchers, a clan that would send four of their own (George, Frank and Bill) to the NHL.

Seven decades later, a Russian NHL journeyman named Andrei Kovalenko, playing for the Canadiens, would score the last NHL goal in the building. In between came an eon of memories, most of which were being dredged up on this night.

Shortly after the game ended Dallas GM Bob Gainey and centre Guy Carbonneau cast aside their Texas affiliations to don the Sainte-Flanelle once again. They moved down to ice level and joined a distinguished group that was gathering for a ceremony

Nobody in the building, with the exception of *La Presse* columnist Réjean Tremblay who choreographed the event, was prepared for the simple, but moving, ceremony that would leave most in the audience teary-eyed, and which would prove to be a fitting *adieu* to an arena that had meant so much to so many for so long.

And right in the middle of the ceremony was the man who made most of the memories in the building, Maurice Richard.

Return to the Forum Family

Rocket Richard's split with the Montreal Canadiens continued for 18 years – ironically the length of his playing career – his appearances at the Forum occasional and usually in an unofficial capacity.

But he remained highly visible and extremely popular for his appearances as a player and referee with the Oldtimers' team and his commercials for Grecian Formula hair tint, including the "two minutes for looking so good" ad.

The Canadiens went through several periods of greatness with four Stanley Cup crowns in five years in the late 1960s, and six cups, including four in a row, in the 1970s. While many of the old Canadien greats were visible at the celebrations of the triumphs, one important figure too often was missing: the Rocket.

In a strange coincidence, the man whose career made him a sort of "Siamese twin" to Richard, Gordie Howe, encountered similar problems with his club, the Detroit Red Wings, when he retired in 1971. The Wings named him a vice-president and promised him a say in the operation of the club. But when his duties consisted mainly of appearances on behalf of the team, Howe endured it for two years. Then he jumped at the chance to return to the playing ranks in 1973, joining his sons Mark and Marty with the Houston Aeros of the World Hockey Association.

But the two decades of estrangement between an organization and its most famous employee went past and with various front office changes, the rift healed slowly.

In 1981, Richard signed a long-term promotional contract with Molson Breweries the owners of the Canadiens. He was photographed shaking hands with Irving Grundman, who served as the team's general manager from 1978-83.

When Ronald Corey was named president of the team in 1983, one of his early goals was to improve the club's relations with the players who had forged its stellar history. Under Corey, the Canadiens were at the forefront of an NHL-wide movement to upgrade alumni relations. The Rocket and many from the team's long list of Hall of Famers and stars became part of the scene at the Forum again.

An alumni lounge was opened not far from the Canadiens' dressing room, and many former players were in attendance at the games.

"I enjoyed seeing the guys I had played with on a regular basis, because so many good men had been part of the team," Richard said during a 1994 appearance at The Hockey Hall of Fame in Toronto. *"I enjoyed making a few appearances for Molson's and the Canadiens, especially when my wife could be with me."*

The Rocket pondered a question about his rift with the organization for several minutes.

"I guess I had more trouble learning not to be a hockey player than I did learning to be one," he said. *"I missed playing really bad, and I guess I needed to get away from it all for a time. I did have a lot of fun with the freedom of living my life the way I wanted away from the NHL, but not away from hockey because of the Oldtimers. But it was good to be back around the Forum, too."*

When the final siren sounded, and the game's three stars were announced, Forum work crews rolled out four red carpets. These stretched from the blue lines and across the ice and were joined in a huge square. The house lights dimmed and the Procession of Captains began, each successive team leader taking up a place in the square.

Émile Bouchard, who succeeded the late Toe Blake and Bill Durnan, was first, followed by his replacement, Maurice Richard. Next came Jean Béliveau, Henri Richard, Yvan Cournoyer, Serge Savard, Gainey, Carbonneau, and the current bearer of the Holy C, Pierre Turgeon. On the Canadiens bench, rapt, were three future captains, Mike Keane, Vincent Damphousse and Saku Koivu.

As funereal music played, a torch was lit and handed to Butch Bouchard. He saluted the audience and then moved to his successor, the Rocket. When Maurice Richard brandished the torch, the building erupted in an ovation that had veteran observers shaking their heads and the Rocket in tears. On and on it went, four minutes, six minutes, eight minutes, an incredible wall of sound that cascaded down to ice level in waves for 10 minutes until Maurice could pass the torch on to another great, Jean Béliveau. On a normal evening, Béliveau's accolade would rival the Rocket's, but this crowd was emotionally spent. After four minutes or so of sustained applause for *Gros Bill*, the torch moved on until all captains had flourished it on high.

PUTTING HIS STAMP ON HOCKEY

Maurice Richard and five other hockey greats, were honored by Canada Post with special stamps issued to coincide with the 50th anniversary of the NHL all-star game.

I knew that the Rocket was huge,

I know what the Canadiens mean to this city,

but nothing, nothing at all prepared me for that.

– Mike Keane

^
*Maurice kneels
beside his plaque at
the Madison Square
Garden's Walk of Fame.*

The Class of '61 for the Hockey Hall of Fame was among the most distinguished ever to earn that honor. Maurice Richard, retired but a year, was a member of the class that inaugurated the new hall at Toronto's Exhibition Place.

The Rocket was the first inductee elected to the pantheon within a year of hanging them up. The rules stipulated a normal five-year waiting period between retirement from play and induction. In Rocket's case, however, the selection committee recognized his special status as a player by waiving that regulation and opting for immediate induction.

Some 16 new members entered that year, 10 players, three builders and three officials. Among the players were Milt Schmidt, Syl Apps, Charlie Conacher, Hap Day, George Hainsworth, Joe Hall and Bruce Stuart.

^
Univers Maurice Richard *is a special museum-like display honoring the Rocket. It is located in the Maurice Richard Arena.*

Important honors, other than 14 all-star selections and the Hart Trophy as the National Hockey League's Most Valuable Player, were not new to the Rocket. A few years after entering the hockey hall, he was named to the Canadian Sports Hall of Fame. During his career, he was selected Canadian Athlete of the Year on three occasions in a Canadian Press poll of sports editors.

In Canada's Centennial year of 1967, the Canadian government inaugurated the Order of Canada, to annually honor exemplary Canadians from all walks of life. Among the first group of athletes to receive the award from the Governor General at Rideau Hall in Ottawa was the Rocket, who was nominated as an Officer of the Order of Canada (O.C.) on July 6, and invested on November 24 of that year.

On October 22, 1998, he and fellow Canadien and Officer, Jean Béliveau, returned to Rideau Hall where they were raised in rank to Companion of the Order of Canada (C.C.).

In 1985, he was also invested as officer, Ordre national du Québec.

Sugar Ray Robinson, Ted Kennedy, Clarence Campbell and Jack Sharkey (left), and Jesse Owens, Don Budge and Bobby Jones (right) were some of the major celebrities of the 20th century who shared a dais with Maurice Richard.

Maurice Richard and Prime Minister Jean Chrétien share a moment on the special evening when 3,000 persons from all walks of life honored the Rocket at the Molson Centre.

Never Saw him Play

Mike Keane, sitting on the team bench and not knowing that he, one day, would briefly bear the same C, was drained of emotion after the ceremony.

"I never saw him play, but like many people my age, I heard the stories from my Dad, other relatives and people in that generation," he said.

"I knew that the Rocket was huge, and playing for this team, I know what the Canadiens mean to this city and their fans everywhere. But nothing, nothing at all prepared me for that." Beside him, Turgeon, Damphousse and other players in the Gretzky generation shook their heads in amazement.

"I've spent my whole life in Montreal," added Damphousse, *"but I've never seen anything like this, even when we won the Cup three years ago and the city went nuts."*

The recipient of this outpouring of love and admiration was visibly moved, but less so than those in the current generation of Canadiens. He seemed embarrassed by the ovation, and would admit as much several days later. Journalists who swarmed ice level at ceremony's end for the Rocket's reaction were dismayed to find that he had eschewed the post-ceremony backstage party and had left the building moments after the festivities had wrapped up.

That was quintessential Maurice.

HANDS-ON ART

Maurice Richard and Quebec artist Jean-Paul Riopelle collaborate on a special creation the artist dedicates to his favorite hockey player.

The Trophy

During his illustrious playing career, Rocket Richard often said that the method used to determine the NHL scoring champion, giving goals and assists equal value, was wrong.

"What really mattered was who put the puck in the net," the Rocket once steamed. *"No one remembers who made the passes. Besides, in some NHL cities (especially Detroit), they throw assists around too much. Goals should be what counts."*

The rest of the National Hockey League just needed a few decades to catch up to the Rocket's thinking that goals should really matter.

At the 1999 NHL all-star game in Tampa, the league announced that the Rocket Richard Trophy would be presented each year to the leading goal scorer. Teemu Selanne of the Anaheim Mighty Ducks was the first winner of the award, scoring 46 goals in the 1998-99 season, while Pavel Bure of the Florida Panthers claimed it in 1999-2000 with 56 goals.

The Rocket was in Tampa for the press conference announcing the Montreal Canadiens' donation of the beautiful trophy. It was an emotional time because Richard had fought off stomach cancer discovered a year earlier and looked remarkably healthy that day. The cancer was to claim his life 15 months later.

Talk of a trophy in Richard's honor had been heard for several years, but when his illness was revealed in 1998, Canadiens president **Ronald Corey** led the movement for official recognition of the Rocket's prowess.

"There has never been a goal scorer who galvanized audiences like Maurice Richard, although we have seen tremendous talents like Phil Esposito, Guy Lafleur, Mike Bossy, Wayne Gretzky and Mario Lemieux come and go since Rocket retired," he said.

"Had the trophy existed over the years, all five of those names would have been on it, and in multiple cases. The Maurice Richard Trophy, once established, will become one of the most exciting awards given out at the end of each season."

With the Montreal media on the bandwagon, and with some out-of-town journalists like sportscaster Gord Miller of The Sports Network in Canada leading boosters of the idea, it took very little to convince NHL commissioner Gary Bettman and the league to go ahead, especially after Corey presented Bettman with a petition carrying more than 200,000 signatures.

The trophy was designed and built by a Montreal firm *Au Cœur Du Bronze*, which had created the statue of the Rocket in front of Maurice Richard Arena in Montreal. Made of bronze, silver, wood and brass, the trophy weighs 30 pounds with 50 nameplates, representing the Rocket's 50 goals in 50 games in 1944-45, and has nine levels (No. 9), the Canadiens' red, white and blue colors, a façade of the old Montreal Forum, his motto "never give up" in French and English, and a statue of Richard.

"There were players who scored more goals than I did, but I'm glad they used my name on it," the Rocket said that day.

Thus, reality was added to the mystique of the Rocket, 40 years after he scored his last goal.

CHAPTER 8

"I appreciated the applause – who wouldn't? – but sometimes I wonder what they were applauding," he said two days later, forever the pragmatist.

"I've been retired for 36 years now, it wasn't even their fathers who saw me play, but their grandfathers! I think the fans on that night were applauding the building and the Stanley Cup banners, and I appreciate that because to me, winning was everything. And we won, much more than the others."

Was he swept away with memories of the building, one that he helped renovate in 1949 with his feats on the ice? Would the Forum's departure leave a void?

"It doesn't mean a thing to me that the Forum is moving," he said, refuting the romanticism wafting into the night from the corner of Atwater and St. Catherine.

"It was the right building for our time, and now the Molson Centre will be the building for today. The only thing that bothers me, is that the public will end up paying far too much to go to hockey games from now on."

I appreciated the applause – who wouldn't? – but sometimes I wonder what they were applauding.

— Maurice Richard

Émile Bouchard , Elmer Lach and the Rocket made the trip from the Forum to the Molson Centre.

HOMAGE TO REE-SHARD

By Al Purdy

1976

A two-time Governor General's Award winner, Al Purdy was more at home in a tavern, sitting at a table full of fellow workers in the east-end Angus Shops, a couple quarts of beer lined up in front of him.

He is one of a group of Canadian poets who flaunted their lack of formal education, among them Milton Acorn and Patrick Lane, and whose roots were deeply sunk into blue collar, working-class culture. Purdy's "education" came riding the rods (hitching rides on trains) during the Depression.

He understood better than most what Maurice Richard's success meant to les cols bleus, especially those French-Canadian workers who toiled for English-Canadian bosses all over Montreal.

Born at Wooler, Ont., in 1918, he passed away a couple months before the Rocket. They were kindred spirits.

And then I dreamed and I dreamed Ree-Shard
Ancestor Maurice incestuous mythawful Rocket standing at my bedside
I fled Him down the nights and down the days
I fled Him down the arches of the years
I fled Him down the labyrinthine ways of my own mind – but he was too fast for me
his eyes blazing blowlamps on Décarie and its cloacal hellway and Montreal East kids
with ragged *Canadien* sweaters on St. Germain outside the factory
I worked in all the little Ree-Shards failing to negotiate contact
with their dream among the greasy-spoon cafes and their out of work *pères*
and *mères* among the non-anglos among failed gangsters and busted drug peddlers
and '48 Pontiacs with bad lungs coughing their own smoke in Montreal East
I dreamed Ree-Shard and the kids
Me the failed athlete and failed lover absurd idealist and successful cynic
I dreamed the bitter glory-fled old man nursing his hate and grudges and memories
his balls making only sewer water with Jung and Freud as solemn witnesses
But that man disappeared suddenly and what took his place was the real thing
honest-injun Rocket indubitable Maurice mad mad Ree-Shard
in fact the first and only berserker astronaut among the lesser groundlings
their necessary flyboy who slapped a star along Décarie hellway
and rang a bell at Bonaparte's tomb and knocked a crumb from Antoinette's pastry
waved his wand at Anglos Howe and Ezinicki and made Quebec Canadian

Rocket you'll never read this
but I wish for you all the best things
whatever those may be grow fat drink beer live high off the hog
and may all your women be beautiful
as a black spot of light sailing among the planets
I wish it for just one reason that watching you I know
all the things I knew I couldn't do are unimportant

MAURICE RICHARD

By Félix Leclerc

1983

Born in La Tuque in 1914, Félix Leclerc was a poet, singer, story-teller, and radio dramatist.

Renowned as Quebec's minstrel, Leclerc wove words like only he could in his tales and songs and in a magnificent "Tour de l'Ile" which was published in 1975. His works, written in vivid, evocative language, were inspired by the Québécois milieu, and painted satiric portraits of humanity.

He died on his beloved Ile d'Orleans on August 8, 1988.

Quand il lance, l'Amérique hurle.

Quand il compte, les sourds entendent.

Quand il est puni, les lignes téléphoniques sautent.

Quand il passe, les recrues rêvent.

C'est le vent qui patine.

C'est tout le Québec debout

Qui fait peur et qui vit...

Il neige !

When he shoots, America howls.

When he scores, the deaf hear.

When he is penalized, telephone lines explode.

When he passes, rookies dream.

It's the wind skating.

It's all of Quebec standing

Which frightens and lives…

It's snowing!

THE HOCKEY SWEATER

By Roch Carrier

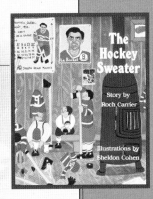

1979

Born in St. Justine, Quebec, in 1937, Roch Carrier was appointed as the fourth National Librarian of the National Library of Canada on October 1, 1999. He has published several stories and novels, all while maintaining a career in education and public administration. In 1979, The Hockey Sweater appeared, a short story and homage to Maurice Richard for which he also wrote a screen treatment for the National Film Board. The excerpt here describes the anguish of a young boy and ferocious fan of the Rocket who, is obliged by unfortunate circumstances, to wear the sweater of the dreaded Toronto Maple Leafs.

I remember very well the winter of 1946. We all wore the same uniform as Maurice Richard, the red, white and blue uniform of the Montreal Canadiens, the best hockey team in the world. We all combed our hair like Maurice Richard, and to keep it in place we used a kind of glue – a great deal of glue. We laced our skates like Maurice Richard, we taped our sticks like Maurice Richard. We cut his pictures out of all the newspapers. Truly, we knew everything there was to know about him.

On the ice, when the referee blew his whistle the two teams would rush at the puck; we were five Maurice Richards against five other Maurice Richards, throwing themselves on the puck. We were ten players all wearing the uniform of the Montreal Canadiens, all with the same burning enthusiasm. We all wore the famous number 9 on our backs.

How could we forget that!

THE ROCKET'S
LAST ROAD TRIP

"I am just a hockey player."

Preparing to move from the Forum to the ultra-

modern Molson Centre, the Montreal Canadiens

struck precisely the correct note with the theme,

Passing the Torch. **9**

The Original and the Space Age:
Maurice Richard has left behind his
original sweater (above) in his passing, but there always will be a No. 9
hockey sweater in Montreal. The
Montreal Rocket, named after
Richard, contains a stylized 9 in its
team logo. No player on the Rocket
will ever wear the No. 9 on the back
of his sweater, however. The team's
first game in the Quebec Major
Junior A Hockey League took place
on September 9, 1999, or 9-9-99.

The stirring closing ceremony after the Forum's final game saw the torch of Colonel John McCrae's *In Flanders Fields* passed among the surviving team captains to resurface four days later in the new building. The poem, perhaps the most poignant written on a battlefield, spoke of thousands of Canadian soldiers who perished in Belgium during the First World War. Perhaps pretentiously, two third-stanza lines were posted high in the Canadiens' dressing room for six decades. But, as the Canadiens won repeatedly over time, the tradition of the torch blended with the CH, and the power of those two lines, grew:

> *"To you from failing hands we throw*
> *The Torch; be yours to hold it high."*

This was the second-most important citation to emanate from the hallowed changing room of the Sainte-Flanelle.

"I am just a hockey player," spoken by Maurice Richard, was the first.

Colonel McCrae's words would have had no effect, no mythology, no meaning, without Maurice Richard's exploits in the 1940s and '50s. The Rocket single-handedly resurrected a team in the depths, built it up into a vehicle of pride and validation for French Canada, and served as Big Brother to the Made-in-Quebec talent parade in his wake, players named Béliveau, Plante, Geoffrion, Talbot, Goyette, Cournoyer, Lemaire, Lafleur, Roy.

> The Torch; be yours to hold it high.
>
> – Colonel John McCrae

Many others from other walks of Quebec life saw this man as a social phenomenon and sought to recruit him to many different causes.

"I am just a hockey player," he respectfully demurred.

In reality, Maurice Richard was the torch, the burning light of a people's soul. When French Canada sought to emerge into the Post-war Era, the exploits of a hockey player provided focus, pride and determination for many of his compatriots. French Canada could not be diminished when he soared fastest and highest in the hockey world.

"Superstar", "symbol", and "cultural icon" are terms used far too loosely. But Maurice Richard was all those things, the Real Deal.

"I am just a hockey player."

And now, in the year 2000, the Rocket was called to a higher arena.

The last decade of Rocket's century was difficult. The 1990s had hardly started when his beloved Lucille became seriously ill. Lucille and Maurice shared their fiftieth wedding anniversary with their seven children in 1992 and, two years later, she passed away, leaving a large void in his life. That was partially filled by Sonia Raymond, the family friend (Huguette) who had cared for Lucille in her final, valiant, struggle, and who would become Maurice's companion in his last years. Her contribution to his well-being was very evident in 1998 when the Rocket was diagnosed with cancer.

The Rocket took part in a special Prostate Cancer Awareness program in 1990, travelling across Canada to counsel middle-aged Canadian men as to the benefits of annual prostatic examinations. It was a poignant sponsorship as the disease had killed his father Onésime several years earlier. Joining Maurice at the campaign launch are Claude Seurret, president of Schering Canada, and Dr. Jean Dupont (left).

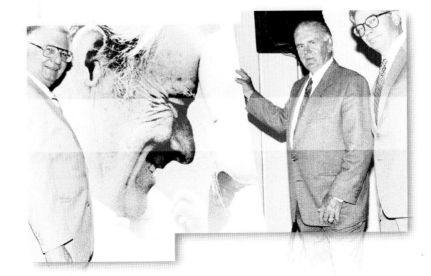

People from all walks of life, and from all over North America, are among the 115,000 well-wishers who visit the Molson Centre to pay their final respects to Maurice Richard on May 30. The line of people passing by the casket would not abate for 24 hours.

It stretched a full city block around the Windsor Station complex.

A tent erected in the Windsor Station courtyard is where the fans left their personal notes and flowers for this special hero.

Lying in State

The illness accelerated the world around the Rocket. When more than 3,000 friends honored him at a special Molson Centre evening, good wishes came via satellite and telegram from Queen Elizabeth II, Wayne Gretzky, Jack Nicklaus, Senator Edward Kennedy, Elvis Stojko, and others. Three weeks later, a two-part television special, *Maurice Richard, Histoire d'un Canadien,* was aired on Radio-Canada in November, 1999.

Richard's health rebounded that winter but in early May took a down-swing, and at 5:40 p.m. on Saturday, May 27, Maurice Richard breathed his last.

Joseph Henri Maurice Richard's passing, like his hockey career, was unique. Headlines of *Adieu, Rocket* emerged the next morning in papers around the world, and the Molson Centre, City Hall and media outlets were besieged by many thousands of calls: Where can we pay our last respects?

It was agreed that the Rocket would be the third person to lie in state at the team's arena – visitation for Howie Morenz and Frank Selke had taken place at the Forum. On May 30, the Rocket was exposed at ice level at the Molson Centre, and the people came. In a line stretching outside the Centre and around the adjacent Windsor Station, more than 115,000 persons would pass the flower-draped casket, including the Montreal Rocket junior team, the club Maurice Richard had helped launch the previous September. Thousands signed a special display in a tent raised in the courtyard of Windsor Station and added to a huge bank of flowers. At the Maurice Richard Arena across town, the bronze statue of the Rocket was draped with hockey sweaters, flags, posters, notes and flowers.

"I am just a hockey player."

But those countless tributes were just the foundation for the May 31 funeral. Thousands upon thousands, ten to twenty deep in some spots, lined the downtown streets taken by the funeral procession from the Molson Centre to the magnificent Notre-Dame church in Old Montreal, and gave Maurice Richard the standing ovation of his life. More than three thousand gathered at the church, and several thousand followed the cortege on foot.

The Montreal Expos found a unique way to pay tribute to hockey legend Maurice Richard after his death – by sewing his famed number "9" on the right sleeve of both their home and away uniforms for the remainder of the 2000 season. It marked the first time in major league baseball history that an athlete from another sport had been so honored. At season's end, the number "9" uniform of first baseman Lee Stevens was donated to the Hockey Hall of Fame.

"Maurice Richard is a giant in every sense of the word. He was an extraordinary star in the hockey world and remains a legendary hero for Montreal, Quebec and the entire country," *said team owner Jeffrey Loria when the announcement was made June 1.* "Honoring him this way is not only appropriate, but shows the proper respect. It will be with tremendous pride that our players adorn his number throughout the league for the rest of this season."

The casket exits Notre-Dame accompanied by eight of the Rocket's teammates, including his brother, Henri, and followed by Msgr. Jean-Claude Turcotte and the Richard family.

The Rocket's teammates inaugurate another team bench on this solemn occasion.

The world of politics, one which the Rocket scrupulously avoided in his lifetime, is well represented, as Prime Minister Jean Chrétien, Quebec Premier Lucien Bouchard, Montreal Mayor Pierre Bourque and members of federal, provincial and municipal cabinets, are in attendance.

Three 20th century Quebec giants, Premiers René Lévesque, Robert Bourassa and Montreal's fabled Mayor Jean Drapeau had been laid to rest with thousands of compatriots present, but nothing in recent memory compared with the Rocket's funeral. The Prime Minister of Canada, the Premier of Quebec, various members of both cabinets, and the hockey world, filled the Notre-Dame pews.

"I am just a hockey player."

The pallbearers, brother Henri, and teammates Elmer Lach, Jean Béliveau, Dickie Moore, Ken Mosdell, Gerry McNeil, Butch Bouchard and Kenny Reardon, reflected the emotions of the thousands gathered at the doors of the church.

As smiles mixed with tears on this day, the Requiem Mass was a Richardian hat trick — the moving and eloquent testimony of family and friends, the sublime rendition of *Ceux qui s'en vont* (Those who leave) by chanteuse Ginette Reno, and the brilliant homily offered by Msgr. Jean-Claude Turcotte whose allusions to fishing and The Fisherman (Jesus) would have earned a smile from the Rocket, an inveterate angler.

Somewhere, the Rocket looked on with a few friends, Frank Selke, Dick Irvin and Toe Blake, Jacques Plante and Bill Durnan, Jean-Claude Tremblay, Claude Provost and Murph Chamberlain.

"I am just a hockey player," he said for the last time.

The world begged to differ.

> *I am just a hockey player.*
>
> – *Maurice Richard, 1921-2000*

Editor's Note

We have made every effort to trace the ownership of copyrighted photos. If we have failed to give adequate credit, we will be pleased to make changes in future printings.

Photos are detailed from left to right, top to bottom on the page they appear. Photographer's name is listed in italics. Source of photo, if differing from author or copyright publication, appears in parentheses. Year photo taken is listed, if known.

Abbreviations

CMR: Maurice Richard Collection
CHC: Canadien Hockey Club
HHOF: Hockey Hall of Fame
BBS: Bruce Bennett Studios
TPP: Team Power Publishing

P.1 MAURICE RICHARD VS. THE MAPLE LEAFS, 1955, *David Bier,* ©David Bier/CHC

P.2-3 ROCKET'S RED GLARE, *David Bier,* ©David Bier/CHC

DICK IRVIN & TEAM, *David Bier,* ©David Bier/CHC

MAURICE RICHARD WITH CUP, *Turofsky,* ©Imperial Oil-Turofsky/HHOF

ALL-STAR GAME, 1956, *David Bier* (Eleonor Kirshner Collection), ©CHC

NUMBER 9, 2000, *Guy Tessier,* ©TPP

P.5 See credits for opening of chapters

P.6 MAURICE & HENRI RICHARD, 1956, (Eleonor Kirshner Collection), ©CHC

HENRI RICHARD, 1993, *Bob Fisher,* ©Bob Fisher/CHC

P.7 MAN WITH FLAG, 2000, *Ladislav Kadyszewski,* ©Kadyszewski/CHC

PIERRE BOIVIN, ©CHC

P.8 MAURICE RICHARD, 1994, *Bob Fisher,* ©Bob Fisher/CHC

CHAPTER 1

P.10-11 MAURICE RICHARD ENTERING, ©La Presse

HENRI & CLAUDE RICHARD PLAYING HOCKEY, 1943, (Rollande Richard), ©G. Depelteau Vallée Collection

M. RICHARD FROM CLUB PAQUETTE, (Rollande Richard), ©G. Depelteau Vallée Collection

CANADIEN VS. RANGERS, 1944, ©BBS

ONÉSIME RICHARD, (Georgette Richard), ©G. Depelteau Vallée Collection

RICHARD FAMILY HOME, (Georgette Richard), ©G. Depelteau Vallée Collection

P.12 MAURICE RICHARD, ©CMR

P.13 DICK IRVIN, circa 1944, ©HHOF

P.14 YOUNG MAURICE RICHARD, ©Imperial Oil-Turofsky/HHOF

MAURICE RICHARD WITH FANS, 1957, *John Taylor,* ©La Presse

MAURICE WITH PAPER, ©CMR

P.15 1945-46 CANADIENS, *David Bier,* ©David Bier/CHC

MONTREAL FORUM CIRCA 1950, ©CHC

P.17 BABY MAURICE RICHARD, (Rollande Richard), ©G. Depelteau Vallée Collection

MAURICE & SISTER GEORGETTE WITH PARENTS, (Georgette Richard), ©G. Depelteau Vallée Collection

MAURICE WITH PARENTS, (Rollande Richard), ©G. Depelteau Vallée Collection

P.18 PAQUETTE JUNIOR HOCKEY TEAM, ©CMR

MAURICE RICHARD WITH P.-É. PAQUETTE, (Rollande Richard), ©G. Depelteau Vallée Collection

P.19 1030-31 CANADIENS, *Jimmy Rice,* ©Chrys Goyens Collection

AUREL JOLIAT, ©HHOF

NEWSY LALONDE, *Jimmy Rice,* ©CHC

ACTION HOWIE MORENZ, ©HHOF

P.20 PAQUETTE MIDGET HOCKEY TEAM, ©CMR

P.21 HOCKEY CARD, ©Univers Maurice Richard

P.22 RICHARDS' WEDDING, 1942, ©CHC

RICHARDS ON 50ᵗʰ WEDDING ANNIVERSARY, ©La Presse

THE ROCKET & KIDS WITH TROPHY, 1999, ©Bob Fisher/CHC

LUCILLE & MAURICE RICHARD, ©CMR

MAURICE & LUCILLE POSING, *Bob Fisher,* ©Bob Fisher/CHC

P.23 THE RICHARD KISS, *David Bier,* ©CMR

RICHARDS WITH BABY, ©CMR

RICHARD FAMILY POSING, ©CMR

LUCILLE & MAURICE ON BEACH, ©CMR

P.24 ROCKET IN ACTION, ©CMR

PAUL HAYNES, *David Bier,* ©David Bier/CHC

P.25 ROCKET & ELMER LACH, 1947, ©La Presse

CANADIENS HOCKEY TEAM, ©CMR

P.26 MAURICE RICHARD, ©CMR

P.27 CANADIENS VS. RANGERS, 1944, ©BBS

MAURICE WITH PUCK, ©CMR

STEVE BUZINSKI, ©HHOF

CHAPTER 2

P.28-29 THE CANADIENS CELEBRATING, ©La Presse

VISIT AT THE COLLEGE DE MONTRÉAL, ©CMR

MAURICE RICHARD IN ACTION (all three), ©CMR

LUCILLE & MAURICE, *David Bier,* ©CMR

P.30 ROCKET 100ᵗʰ GOAL VS. BRODA, *Turofsky,* ©Imperial Oil Turofsky/HHOF

P.31 MONTREAL CANADIENS BASEBALL TEAM, ©CMR

P.32 MAURICE RICHARD POSING, *Paul Stuart,* ©La Presse

THE ROCKET IN ACTION, ©La Presse

P.33 THE CANADIENS AT ST. ARSÈNE ORPHANAGE, 1953, *Marcel Desjardins,* ©La Presse

MAURICE SKATING, *Turofsky,* ©Imperial Oil-Turofsky/HHOF

P.34 MAURICE, E.LACH & SONS, *René Julien,* ©La Presse

P.35 DICK IRVIN AND TEAM, *David Bier,* ©David Bier/CHC

MAURICE RICHARD HOLDING SKATES, ©La Presse

SYLVIO MANTHA, *Jimmy Rice,* ©Chrys Goyens Collection

CHARLIE SANDS, 1940, ©CHC

HOCKEY EQUIPMENT, ©La Presse

MAURICE RICHARD FROM THE BACK, *David Bier,* ©David Bier/CHC

P.36 ROCKET AGAINST THE LEAFS, *Turofsky,* ©Imperial Oil-Turofsky/HHOF

MAURICE RICHARD HOLDING PUCK, ©CMR

ROCKET IN RED SWEATER, *Jimmy Rice,* ©CHC

THE CANADIENS CELEBRATING, ©La Presse

P.37 RETIRED PUNCH LINE, *Denis Brodeur,* ©Denis Brodeur

YOUNG PUNCH LINE, *David Bier,* ©CHC

P.38 ROCKET'S RED GLARE, *David Bier,* ©David Bier/CHC

6 ACTION SHOTS, ©CMR

P.39 MAURICE RICHARD WITH ROCKET, ©CMR

COVER LE ROCKET DU HOCKEY, ©CHC

MAURICE RICHARD ON SKATES, *Roger St-Jean,* ©La Presse

P.40 HAT TRICK, *Roger St-Jean,* ©La Presse

MAURICE RICHARD WITH TROPHY, 1967, ©La Presse

ROCKET SCORING, *David Bier,* ©David Bier/CHC

P.41 ROCKET WITH HAT, *Albert Giroux,* ©CMR

P.42 ROCKET & TOE BLAKE, ©CMR

RICHARD VS. RANGERS, ©BBS

P.43 MAURICE WITH STICK, ©HHOF

1943-44 CANADIENS, *David Bier,* ©David Bier/CHC

CHAPTER 3

P.44-45 STANLEY CUP CELEBRATION, 1953, *David Bier,* ©David Bier/CHC

FRANK SELKE, ©HHOF

RICHARD & BÉLIVEAU, ©CHC

FRANK SELKE WITH HAT, ©HHOF

MAURICE RICHARD DAY IN TORONTO, *Turofsky,* ©CHC

SENATOR H. MOLSON PRESENTING A GIFT, 1958, ©La Presse

P.46 MAURICE WITH LOUIS ST. LAURENT, 1949, *Albert Giroux,* ©La Presse

ONÉSIME & MAURICE RICHARD, *Canadian Pacific,* ©La Presse

CANADIENS WITH CAMILIEN HOUDE, 1946, ©La Presse

P.47 RICHARD & SELKE, *Adolphe,* ©CMR

P.48 BILL DURNAN & THE ROCKET, (CHC), ©La Presse

RICHARD VS. JACQUES PLANTE, 1957, ©La Presse

CANADIENS VS. RANGERS, ©CHC

RICHARD VS. TERRY SAWCHUK, 1956, ©La Presse

WALTER TURK BRODA, *Imperial Oil,* ©HHOF

P.49 CANADIENS VS. RED WINGS, ©CHC

P.50 1956 STANLEY CUP DINNER AT CITY HALL, ©Jean Béliveau Collection

P.51 ROCKET & KIDS ON SLEDGE, *G. A. Laferrière,* ©CMR

E. LACH & RICHARD WITH SONS, *René Julien,* ©CMR

MAURICE RICHARD WITH WIFE & DAUGHTERS, 1959, *Roger St-Jean,* ©La Presse

P.52 CANADIENS VS. MAPLE LEAFS, *Turofsky,* ©Imperial Oil-Turofsky/HHOF

TED LINDSAY, *Turofsky,* ©Imperial Oil-Turofsky/HHOF

TED LINDSAY IN DRESSING ROOM, *Turofsky,* ©Imperial Oil-Turofsky/HHOF

BILL GADSBY, *Turofsky,* ©Imperial Oil-Turofsky/HHOF

RED KELLY, ©HHOF

P.53 BOOM BOOM GEOFFRION & THE ROCKET, 1954, ©La Presse

P.54 MAURICE RICHARD, ©BBS

P.55 THE ROCKET & TOE BLAKE, *Turofsky,* ©Imperial Oil-Turofsky/HHOF

ÉMILE BOUCHARD, *David Bier,* ©David Bier/CHC

P.56 THE ROCKET SKATING, *David Bier,* ©CMR

THE 1946-47 CANADIENS, *Tim Rice,* ©CMR

P.57 RICHARD & TEAMMATES, *Frank Prazak,* ©Frank Prazak/HHOF

NEWSY LALONDE & MAURICE RICHARD, 1956, ©La Presse

CANADIENS IN DRESSING ROOM, 1948, *Réal St-Jean,* ©La Presse

JACQUES PLANTE, *David Bier,* ©David Bier/CHC

CANADIENS 1950, ©CMR

CHAPTER 4

P.58-59 RICHARD & HOWE WITH KIDS, *Denis Brodeur,* ©Denis Brodeur

RED WINGS VS. CANADIENS, ©BBS

HOWE & RICHARD SITTING, *Denis Brodeur,* ©Denis Brodeur

MAURICE RICHARD HOLDING PUCK, *United Press,* ©CMR

MAURICE RICHARD SKATING, *David Bier,* ©CMR

GORDIE HOWE SKATING, ©London Life-Portnoy/HHOF

M. RICHARD FROM BACK, 1955, *David Bier,* ©David Bier/CHC

P.60 ROCKET & YVON ROBERT, ©CMR

P.61 THE ROCKET VS. MAPLE LEAFS, ©Imperial Oil-Turofsky/HHOF

P.62 1949 ALL-STAR TEAM, ©CMR

P.63 RICHARD AT THE BLACKBOARD, ©La Presse

MAURICE RICHARD WITH TROPHY, 1951, ©La Presse

THE ROCKET WITH PUCKS, ©CMR

P.64 LACH, RICHARD, THOMSON & KENNEDY, 1954, ©La Presse

P.65 MAURICE RICHARD & RED STOREY, ©CHC

P.66 LACH & RICHARD HOLDING CUP, 1953, *David Bier,* ©David Bier/CHC

LACH, RICHARD & BOUCHARD CELEBRATING, 1953, *David Bier,* © David Bier/CHC

P.67 STANLEY CUP, ©HHOF

LACH & RICHARD EMBRACING, 1953, *David Bier,* ©David Bier/CHC

P.68 CANADIENS VS. RED WINGS, *David Bier,* ©David Bier/CHC

P.69 NORMAND & MAURICE RICHARD, 1957, ©La Presse

M. RICHARD CARRIED BY CROWD, 1954, *Jacques Doyon,* ©CMR

M. RICHARD, É. GENEST & P. VALCOUR, 1954, ©La Presse

CROWD AT THE WINDSOR STATION, 1954, *David Bier,* ©CMR

P.70 THE ROCKET & SUGAR JIM HENRY, 1952, *Roger St-Jean,* ©La Presse

HISTORICAL GOAL MONTREAL VS. BOSTON, 1952, *David Bier,* ©CHC

ROCKET & SENATOR DONAT RAYMOND, 1952, ©La Presse

P.71 RICHARD & TEAMMATES, *Turofsky,* ©Imperial Oil-Turofsky/HHOF

RED HENRY & RICHARD IN ACTION, *David Bier,* ©David Bier/CHC

P.72 HOWE & RICHARD SITTING, *Denis Brodeur,* ©Denis Brodeur

P.73 MAURICE & HENRI RICHARD, 1956, (Eleonor Kirshner Collection), ©CHC

RICHARD BROTHERS & DICKIE MOORE, ©HHOF

HENRI RICHARD WITH CUPS, 1993, *Bob Fisher,* ©Bob Fisher/CHC

P.74-75 MAURICE RICHARD VS. THE MAPLE LEAFS, 1955, *David Bier,* ©David Bier/CHC

CHAPTER 5

P.76-77 BOMB EXPLODES AT THE FORUM, 1955, *David Bier,* ©David Bier/CHC

THE ROCKET VS. THE RANGERS, *David Bier,* ©David Bier/CHC

MAURICE RICHARD IN SUIT, *David Bier,* ©CMR

THE FORUM, THE DAY AFTER THE RIOT, 1955, ©La Presse

ST. CATHERINE STREET AFTER THE RIOT, 1955, ©La Presse

MAURICE RICHARD WITH HAT, 1955, *Roger St-Jean,* ©La Presse

P.78 CANADIENS VS. BLACKHAWKS, ©CHC

THE ROCKET VS. THE MAPLE LEAFS, (HHOF), ©Michael Burns

P.79 RICHARD, GORMAN, LACH & BLAKE, 1955, ©La Presse

P.80 HUGH MACLENNAN, ©McGill University Archives

ACTION CANADIENS VS. MAPLE LEAFS, ©BBS

P.81 RICHARD WITH FANS, ©CMR

MAURICE RICHARD SIGNING AUTOGRAPHS, ©CMR

P.84 REFEREE FRANK UDVARI, ©Frank Udvari

BRUINS VS. CANADIENS & REFEREE, 1955, *Herbert Capwell,* ©Frank Udvari

RICHARD KNEELING WITH REFEREES, ©Imperial Oil-Turofsky/HHOF

REFEREE RED STOREY, ©HHOF

P.85 JACQUES PLANTE, 1957, *Turofsky,* ©Imperial Oil-Turofsky/HHOF

RED STOREY & MAURICE RICHARD AS REFEREES, 1979, *Armand Trottier,* ©La Presse

MAURICE RICHARD IN REFEREE, *Graphic Artists,* ©HHOF

YOUNG FRANK UDVARI, *Turofsky,* ©Frank Udvari

BILL CHADWICK, ©BBS

P.86 MAURICE RICHARD IN SUIT, *David Bier,* ©CMR

P.87 BOOM BOOM GEOFFRION & MAURICE RICHARD, 1955, ©La Presse

P.88-89 CLARENCE CAMPBELL AT DESK, 1955, ©CMR

DICK IRVIN & MAURICE RICHARD, 1955, *Roger St-Jean,* ©La Presse

KENNY REARDON & MAURICE RICHARD, 1955, ©La Presse

JOURNALISTS AT THE DOOR, 1955, ©CMR

P.90 HENRI & MAURICE RICHARD, *Turofsky,* ©Imperial Oil-Turofsky/HHOF

P.91 MAURICE & BOOM BOOM GEOFFRION, *Denis Brodeur,* ©Denis Brodeur

AUTHORS' ACKNOWLEDGEMENTS

We wish to thank the following for their special participation and contributions: Evelyn Armstrong, Jean Béliveau, Denis Dion, Anne Fotheringham, Henri Richard, Jean Roy and Terry Scott.

Outside special contributors who rallied around the project include Bruce Bennett, Bob Borgen, Denis Brodeur, Gordon Burr, Louise Fagnan, Roland Forget, Dominique Jacques, Philip Norton, Phil Pritchard, Guy Tessier and Frank Udvari. We would also like to thank Jacques Martineau of the *Univers Maurice Richard* for his contribution, as well as Monique Giroux and Sina Gabrieli of the Montreal Expos Baseball Club and Christian Simoneau of the Montreal Rocket Hockey Club of the QMJHL.

Last, and definitely most, this book could not and would not be what it is without the very special contributions of Julie Desilets and Geneviève Desrosiers. Lending a precious hand in their everyday endeavors were Nathalie Michaud and Patrick Dupuis.

BIBLIOGRAPHY | SOURCES

Behind the Cheering, by Frank J. Selke with Gordon Green, McClelland & Stewart, Toronto, 1962.

Jean Béliveau, My Life in Hockey, by Jean Béliveau with Chrys Goyens and Allan Turowetz, McClelland & Stewart, Toronto, 1994.

Blades on Ice, A Century of Professional Hockey, by Chrys Goyens and Frank Orr, Team Power Enterprises, Toronto, 1999.

Boom Boom, The Life and Times of Bernard Geoffrion, by Bernard Geoffrion and Stan Fischler, McGraw Hill-Ryerson Ltd., Whitby, Ont., 1997.

Firewagon Hockey, The Story of the Montreal Canadiens, by Andy O'Brien, The Ryerson Press, Toronto, 1967.

Forever Rivals, Montreal Canadiens – Toronto Maple Leafs, James Duplacey, Charles Wilkins, edited by Dan Diamond, Dan Diamond and Associates, Inc., Toronto, 1996.

Gordie: A Hockey Legend, by Roy MacSkimming, Greystone Books, a division of Douglas & McIntyre Ltd, Vancouver, 1994.

The Habs, An Oral History of the Montreal Canadiens, 1940-1980, by Dick Irvin, McClelland & Stewart, Toronto, 1991.

The Hockey Sweater, by Roch Carrier, Tundra Books, a division of McClelland & Stewart, Toronto, 1979.

Hockey, The Official Book of the Game, Hamlyn Publishing, London, 1980.

100 Great Moments in Hockey, by Brian Kendall, Viking (Penguin Books Canada Ltd.) Toronto, 1994.

In the Crease, Goaltenders Look at Life in the NHL, by Dick Irvin, McClelland & Stewart, 1995.

The Leafs, An Anecdotal History of the Toronto Maple Leafs, by Jack Batten, Key-Porter Books, Toronto, 1994.

Lions in Winter, by Chrys Goyens and Allan Turowetz, Prentice-Hall, Toronto, 1986.

Lions in Winter, Revised edition, by Chrys Goyens and Allan Turowetz, McGraw-Hill Ryerson, Toronto, 1993.

The Mad Men of Hockey, by Trent Frayne, McClelland & Stewart, Toronto, 1974.

Maurice Richard : l'idole d'un peuple, Revised edition, by Jean-Marie Pellerin, Éditions Trustar, Montreal, 1998.

The Montreal Canadiens, An Illustrated History of a Hockey Dynasty, by Claude Mouton, Key Porter, Toronto, 1987.

The Montreal Forum, Forever Proud, by Chrys Goyens, with Allan Turowetz and Jean-Luc Duguay, Les Éditions Effix Inc., Montreal, 1996.

Howie Morenz, Hockey's First Superstar, by Dean Robinson, Boston Mills Press, Erin, Ont., 1982.

National Hockey League 75th Anniversary Commemorative Book, Edited by Dan Diamond, McClelland & Stewart, Toronto, 1991.

Remembering The Rocket, edited by Craig MacInnis, Stoddart Publishing, Toronto, 1998.

Red's Story, Red Storey with Brodie Snyder, Macmillan of Canada, Toronto, 1994.

Rocket Richard, by Andy O'Brien, The Ryerson Press, Toronto, 1961.

Total Hockey, The Official Encyclopedia of the National Hockey League, Total Sports (Dan Diamond and Associates), New York, 1998.

The Trail of the Stanley Cup, Volume 1, 1893-1926 inc., by Charles S. Coleman, National Hockey League Publications, 1966.

The Trail of the Stanley Cup, Volume 2, 1927-1946 inc., by Charles S. Coleman, National Hockey League Publications, 1969.

The Trail of the Stanley Cup, Volume 3, 1947-1967 inc., by Charles S. Coleman, National Hockey League Publications, 1976.

Years of Glory, 1942-1967, The National Hockey League's Official Book of the Six-Team Era, edited by Dan Diamond, McClelland & Stewart, Toronto, 1994.

Maclean's Magazine, Toronto

Sports Illustrated, New York

The New Yorker, New York

The Miami Herald, Miami, Fla.

Le Journal de Montréal, Montreal

Documentation La Presse, Montreal

Montréal-Matin, Montreal

City of Montreal Public Library

The Toronto Star, Toronto

The Hockey News